FORTUNE, FAMILY, FRACTURE

A New York Story

Also by Robert J. Hooper

Finding Grace, *Meandering through the Life and Writings of Grace Duncan Hooper*

Born to Responsibility, *Remembering New York's Little Mothers*

FORTUNE, FAMILY, FRACTURE

A NEW YORK STORY

ROBERT J. HOOPER

Meripoint
Books

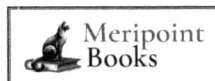

Notice: The information in this book is true to the best of our knowledge. It is offered without guarantee on the part of the author or Meripoint Books. The author and Meripoint Books disclaim all liability in connection with the use of this book.

Cover design by ML Brei. Credits: Library of Congress, Geography and Map Division; Currier & Ives. *The city of New York*. New York, Currier & Ives, 1870. Map. https://www.loc.gov/item/75694809/. Photograph of John Hooper: private collection of Hooper & Brei families.

First published 2025

Manufactured in the United States of America

Paperback 978-1-960808-13-4
Hardcover 978-1-960808-14-1

Meripoint Books LLC
www.meripointbooks.com

Meripoint Books

Dedication

To Ellen, captivating me for more than 42 years.

CONTENTS

Prologue

John Hooper would have said he was built for the 19th Century. After losing his father in infancy, John grew into a young man able to obtain a formidable education that allowed him to navigate the evolving business, political, and moral issues in his native New York City from 1840 to 1889. These were tumultuous times marked by slavery, territorial expansion, the horrific Civil War, and its lingering aftermath. This was also a time of rapid population growth, industrial expansion, poverty, and the emergence of malicious street gangs.

These times helped define John, who forged through it all with a multifaceted career that spanned four decades beginning before the Civil War and ending when the Gilded Age was blossoming in his beloved New York. He apparently seldom traveled far, but so much of what he touched during his local New York journey was better off for his being there.

John was foremost an entrepreneur. What he touched in his business life succeeded, and he did so with little fanfare. He stepped on few toes, but was ready to square off when his dignity was threatened. As a man of firsts, John seemed to relish risk, stepping carefully through potential hazards and keeping his eye on the rewards.

John's ambitions seemed boundless. He was ready to take on more responsibilities and seemed to be the first to indicate he could and would do whatever the task at hand required. This would include political interests spanning the critical mid-century decades of the 1840s to the 1880s. John along with a powerful friend were swept up in the anti-slavery sentiment growing in New York City.

Beyond his professional accomplishments, John embodied the values of the 19th-century family man. Always the generous provider and resolute protector, John was remarkably successful in eliminating any wants. His wife, Angeline, a formidable daughter of the American Revolution, managed household expenses and cared for their three children. She was the glue that held their family together.

As his success grew, John donated generously to a large number of charities each year. However, he was aware that his wealth attracted individuals seeking benevolence. And his assent would be hard to come by, especially when it came to his lovely daughters, the head-strong Mary Louise and his youngest, the demure Henrietta Frances.

To this end, John Hooper updated his will for the last time on March 5, 1889. Circumstances involving his family had been altered irretrievably and his will would embrace that change. This final document was lengthy and tediously explained the whys and why nots of his decision-making, while providing for disposition of $5 million dollars in assets acquired over his remarkable life. Other than a few scraps of information, John's will was all that was initially available in an attempt to understand his intriguing life and the challenging circumstances he navigated during his lifetime.

The sixteen chapters devoted to understanding his life and how he shaped and was shaped by his times, suggest that while not a giant in this era, he was remarkably impactful and consequential. He was the type of man who embraced the tumult that marked the mid- to late-19th Century. He was incredibly successful and was devoted to his many business enterprises, his politics, family, and the charities he loved. With each step of his journey, John left behind enduring legacies. Knowing a little about his life and its twists and turns uniquely illuminates the hustle and bustle of 19th-century New York City. It was a delightful journey for this writer and hopefully the reader as well. Together we can answer the the final question, at the end was John Hooper willful or heartbroken?

CHAPTER 1

John Hooper Dies

For what shall it profit a man, if he shall gain the
whole world, and lose his own soul?[1]

It was the Fourth Sunday of Advent, nearly Christmastide,
when John Hooper succumbed to a heart valve failure in his
home on December 22, 1889. He was 73 years, 3 months and
3 days old.[2] As was atypical for that time of year, the day was
clear, dry and warm for December. Indeed, Christmas was a
scant three days away, yet the City had a recorded
temperature of 65 degrees and was the "warmest ever known
in this vicinity in December and 13 degrees higher than any
previous Christmas."[3] While the trees lining Brooklyn streets
had lost their foliage, the City was nevertheless festooned

---

[1] Mark 8:36 (from the Bible owned by his grandson, John Stanley Hooper)

[2] Green-Wood.com

[3] Brooklyn Eagle, December 31, 1889

with the joy and mirth of the upcoming season. Brooklyn was sprinkled with Christmas Markets offering everything from Christmas candies, fruits and assorted presents to be purchased for the season.

Brooklyn Christmas Market, 1889

On this late December Sunday, New Yorkers and Brooklynites would have started their day with coffee and a morning paper. Soon, the streets would have been bristling with after-Church shoppers eager to complete their Christmas shopping, especially enjoying the inviting and peculiar balmy winter weather.

That Sunday, at least one newspaper may have featured the continuing saga of Nellie Bly's (Elizabeth Jane Cochrane) trip around the world in less than eighty days. Nellie, a spry 25-year-old from Pittsburgh, had begun her journey in

Nellie Bly (Library of Congress)

November, and on December 27, 1889, would be traversing from Hong Kong to "Frisco" on the steamship Oceanic.[4] Her publisher, Joseph Pulitzer, was looking to push newspaper sales with this stunt. Nellie had already captured the attention of New Yorkers with her daring exposé, *Ten Days in a Mad-House* (1887). A trip around the world, wearing one outfit, was certainly a daunting task, but Nellie was up for the challenge.

As for John Hooper, he had always loved the Christmas season and "[i]t was his invariable custom at Christmas time to send a check to each of the charitable organizations in this city."[5] Indeed "[o]ne of the last acts of his life was to draw a number of checks for various charitable institutions to which he was a regular contributor."[6] While suffering with heart complications, he nonetheless died unexpectedly in his recently acquired home in Brooklyn. As described by one obituarist, John's residence "was a handsomely furnished house at 281 Madison Street."[7] His home would have been decked with garlands and have included a notable Christmas tree burdened with ornaments. Henrietta would have seen to this, as the only remaining daughter still living at home. No doubt her married siblings would have carried on the family

---

[4] *The Evening World*, December 27, 1889.

[5] *New York Times*, December 23, 1889.

[6] *New York Tribune*, December 23, 1889.

[7] *The Times Union*, December 31,1889.

tradition of sharing and spreading their joy of the season in their own homes.

John Hooper's passing evoked headlines throughout New York and the country, indeed all the way to Seattle. There was no need for the family to write and place an obituary; instead, his many obituaries of all lengths and themes were written by reporters keen on a story. After all, he had once been an important part of the newspaper business and had almost single-handedly changed the way newspapers generated revenue with slick advertising campaigns. But the story angle that captivated New Yorkers and newsreaders all over the country, wasn't his historical attachment to newspaper revenue. Instead the story that consumed the headlines was his suspense-filled Last Will and Testament, which dictated the winners and loser of his world. This was the winning angle, exposing who was in and who was out, that drove most of the headlines.

These stories of course would not obscure the holiday season, but only fueled gossip and speculation to be shared by many of New York's elites at sundry parties throughout the holidays. But for now, the lament was for a man with no tomorrows and a time for reflection on some of his 26,645 yesterdays.

John's funeral was at his home on Christmas Eve. The "simple services" were officiated by Dr. E.P. Ingersoll of the Puritan Congregational Church.[8] The service was "largely attended"[9] by his many friends and associates who perhaps

---

[8] *The Brooklyn Daily Times*, December 24, 1889.
[9] *The Brooklyn Citizen*, December 29, 1899.

discussed some of his yesterdays. Among those in attendance was a Committee from the *Real Estate Exchange,* board members from the Tribune Company, and directors from the Iron Steamboat Company, the Anglo-American Electric Light Company, and the Gibson Light Company. John had served them well and it was time to pay final respects.

Given his generosity over the years, there were also representatives from many charities in attendance. Board members past and present of North River Savings Bank also paid their respects, and George P. Rowell, who succeeded John as owner to an advertising company John created and conducted in spaces on the second floor of the New York Times building, would have attended. It was abundantly clear that John had cut a significant swath throughout New York's business, political and social milieu as he journeyed throughout a life of exploring opportunities and contributing wealth to the communities he served, as well as for his family and himself.

And on an otherwise joyous Christmas Eve, with everyone "in the best of humor, and the bright faces of pretty maidens, with their arms full of packages…"[10] John was laid to rest at Green-Wood, the preeminent cemetery in Brooklyn. His procession was accompanied by only family and close friends.

John Hooper

---

[10] *Brooklyn Eagle*, December 24, 1889.

John's Final Resting Place at Green-Wood Cemetery

CHAPTER 2

Getting Started

It was the first of his 26,000 tomorrows

How does John, the son of George Hooper, an immigrant from England, amass a multi-million dollar fortune before his death in 1889?[11] How did this man, who though orphaned as a child, attend a seminary in Vermont and then the U.S. Military Academy at West Point? How did John dramatically and most successfully change careers every few years, including creating a career out of thin air? How does this man, after the death of his wife and approaching his own mortality, take such rigid control over his daughters? Was he attempting to protect them or had he become heartless and cruel, a schemer and a puppet master over his family? Or was this a symptom of his grief?

---

[11] In 2024 his fortune was worth between $68 million to $171 million. www.officialdata.org.

Long before these questions can be answered, John's story begins with his father, George Hooper. New York City was destined to become a better place because George Hooper emigrated from England to the United States prior to the War of 1812. George arrived with finely honed civil engineering skills, which he had developed while working on the Thames Embankment in England.[12] In New York, he applied his expertise to the design and building of Trinity Church as well as Old St. Patrick's Basilica (formerly the Mott Cathedral); completed in 1815.[13]

Etching of St. Patrick's Old Cathedral-1831 (Wikimedia Commons)

[12] *The Sun*, January 1, 1890.
[13] www.waltergrutchfield.net.

When George made the Atlantic crossing, he brought with him his Scottish wife and their twins, William and Mary, born in 1804. Perhaps in keeping with the Hooper's apparent loyalty to the Crown, their New World children were John, Charles T., and Thomas.

John, the first of these American-born children, was born on September 19, 1816, in New York. His siblings William and Mary, already twelve years his senior, were possibly delighted with his arrival, especially Mary who may have had to share in the duties of carrying for the newborn. Her love for John would be later recounted when John became a father.

And as John's story unfolds, he must first grapple with the untimely death of his father. As recounted in a letter of nomination to West Point, John had lost his father "while in his infancy; by that event he was left without a protector…".[14] Despite being orphaned as late as seven years old, his love of learning and literature shone through: "he delighted in traversing the primrose paths of literature and poetry and thought no time better employed than that devoted to the enlightenment of his mind."[15]

On his own, John seized the opportunities presented to him, even at a young age.[16] John, "by his own exertion and good conduct acquired a very creditable education."[17] And it

---

[14] Letter of Nomination to West Point, February 14, 1835, located in the Library of Congress (courtesy of W. Brei). See Appendix III for the transcription.

[15] *The Brooklyn Citizen*, November 1, 1896.

[16] "infancy" as used in this context probably refers to before the age of knowing, i.e.. 7 years old.

[17] Letter of Nomination, February 14, 1835.

was John who didn't forget his extended family even at the
end of his life.

SCHOOLING

But John's siblings and their progeny would have to wait a
while to reap the bounty of his legacy. John's thousands of
tomorrows had only just begun. He was initially educated in
New York City, but then traveled north to Troy, New York, for
an extended stay with one of his brothers. Soon, nearby
Vermont beckoned with an early opportunity: the chance for
John to attend and board at the newly opened Burr Seminary
in Manchester, Vermont. How John discovered and connected
with this new institution remains a mystery. However, it is
likely that there was sufficient chatter about the seminary
that it reached John while he was staying with his brother in
Troy, given that Manchester was less than sixty miles away.

The seminary was named after Joseph Burr who had
bequeathed $10,000 to establish "a literary institution at
Manchester."[18] His beneficence came with a few conditions:
"that an equal sum of $10,000 should within five years from
his decease, be raised and expended in erecting suitable
buildings...."[19]

What would make the Burr Seminary somewhat unique
was its dual emphasis. On the one hand it would be primarily
a "Charity School, to assist pious youth of fair talents in

---

[18] *Middlebury Free Press*, January 21, 1830.
[19] *The Horn of the Green Mountains.* October 26, 1830

obtaining the earlier part of their education on the way to the Christian Ministry."[20] On the other hand, the school would be a *"Working Institution*, in which poor youth, may in part or in the whole support themselves." (Emphasis original)[21]

The incredible efforts by the Trustees and the community paid off. The *Burr Seminary* was "publicly dedicated on the 15th of May [1833]."[22] "It ha[d] already received about 100 students."[23]

Was John part of the first class? He would have been about 17 years old and primed for education in letters and/or learning working skills, including engineering. His pathway is shrouded in mystery, but he was probably a boarding student. His experience at Burr Seminary would have further refined his "good moral character and correct deportment,"[24] the prerequisites to attending Burr Seminary.

For many seminarians, their time at Burr was a stepping stone to a religious ministry or to a higher education. For John, his next step was back to New York, where he studied at the Troy Polytechnic and then at West Point. Both schools would provide the civil engineering education John needed, at least for a while.

---

[20] *Vermont Chronicle*, March 23, 1832.

[21] Ibid.

[22] *Hartford Courant*, June 3, 1833.

[23] Ibid.

[24] *The Horn of the Green Mountains*, October 26, 1830

Burr Seminary

About 164 miles separate Burr Seminary from West Point. But why would John choose the U.S. Military Academy? For one thing, the Academy was the primary school for civil engineering and topographical engineers in the United States, which took on the tasks of surveying and mapping. It is quite possible John had an aptitude for these rigors given his father's background. Or perhaps John believed he could handle the demanding academic program.

While West Point offered a greater challenge than Burr, it was one of degree. John had already traveled a similar road. Presumably, he had great success at the Burr Seminary. But was he aware that West Point was "the best school in the world"?[25] He may have been equipped with this knowledge.

---

[25] Andrew Jackson, and the title of an excellent scholarly work *The Best School* by James L. Morrison, Jr.

In any event, the prospect of a cadetship would appear to return this young ambitious man back to New York, traveling the 164 miles from Vermont to this unique educational facility.

John still had to be accepted into the Military Academy. It took a concerted effort by men of significant civil and political standing to get the required appointment from Secretary of War, Lewis Cass. It was also a circuitous route involving a munitions manufacturer, a New York Congressman, and perhaps a Vermont Congressmen.

Getting John into West Point began with an earnest letter written by "Gueverneur" Kemble, appropriately the founder of West Point Foundry, a munitions manufacturer that also made locomotives. It is not clear whether John was an employee at the foundry, but Mr. Kemble took time to write his Congressman, Job Pierson, urging John's appointment:

> The undersigned, hereby beg leave to recommend John Hooper as a suitable person to be appointed cadet in the Military Academy at West Point. Mr. Hooper is a young man of good character and exemplary habits, he has been for two years, a student in the Manual Labour Seminary in Manchester, Vermont. From the officers of that institution and from many respectable gentlemen in that vicinity, he has received high testimonials and recommendations.
>
> Those who are intimately acquainted with him, believe him to be particularly well fitted to become a member of a Military Academy,[26]

---

[26] Letter of Nomination to West Point, private collection.

Congressman Pierson was well aware of Gueverneur Kemble, an established gentleman and large employer in his District. With concurrences from additional gentlemen and signatures of more than forty others, the petition was sent to the Secretary of War urging John's appointment.

So with this considerable civil and political muscle being exerted on behalf of a teenager, Congressman Pierson assented to supporting John's candidacy, even though he had never met him. He wrote the following to the Secretary of War:

> It is proper that I should transmit the enclosed recommendation to you. I am well acquainted with the subscribers. They are members of the Senate of New York and gentlemen of high standing. They solicit the appointment of a cadet out of my district and out of my state. I presume that my recommendation would be of no avail. I should be gratified if Mr. Hall who represents Manchester would [recommend] the appointment of Mr. Hooper.[27]

It is not clear whether Congressman Hall ever made the requisite recommendation of John Hooper, but nonetheless, John received his appointment and the rest was up to him. West Point would thus become John's home for at least two years. John's admission date was September 1, 1836. He was listed as being 20 years and five months old and hailed from Vermont. (You can count on the Army for its exactness.)

Attending the "best school" meant rigorous and somewhat mechanical "recitations", a nearly daily recounting by the

[27] Ibid.

cadet about what he had read with prompts from the instructors. Each response was graded and then compiled into a weekly report sent to the superintendent. Monthly reports were then sent to the chief of engineers, with extracts sent to the cadet's parents. These recitations were only part of the academic experience. Twice a year there were general examinations on each subject.[28]

John endured the Academy culture for two years. While he did not finish, there is no indication he failed his academic courses. What about John's deportment? This was an equally critical component to the West Point way of life. There was a strict demerit system at West Point. The demerit system was part of a stringent disciplinary system instituted by Superintendent Thayer. To enforce strict attention to detail and self-discipline, "[t]he authorities relied on an intricate and comprehensive system of punishments and demerits. Demerits…were actually assessments against the cadet's grade in conduct…."[29]

Demerits were classified into eight grades with each offense given a point total. A first grade offense [such as mutinous conduct or unauthorized absence] was punished with ten demerits while an eighth grade offense [such as tardiness to roll call or improperly blacked shoes] was punishable by only two.[30] A *Conduct Roll* was maintained throughout the Academic year. Once a Cadet attained the non-distinction of earning 200 demerits he was declared deficient in his conduct and was recommended for discharge

---

[28] *The Best School*, p 87.

[29] Ibid. page 73.

[30] Ibid.

to the War Department. It's fair to say such recommendations were readily approved and a young man's appointment would suddenly end.

So how did John behave? He didn't do as well as some of his famed classmates. Pierre Gustave Toutant (PGT) Beauregard had zero demerits and is widely known as the Confederate General who "started the Civil War at Fort Sumter". On the other side of that great schism was William Tecumseh Sherman, who was assessed with only 66 demerits.[31] As for John, he suffered more than double Sherman's total earning 133 demerits. Not enough for a recommended expulsion but no doubt enough to be noticed!

There is also no indication John was expelled for committing a "single grave crime such as drinking or consorting with prostitutes; [who] faced dismissal by court-martial regardless of his previous conduct record."[32] It is also unlikely he was one of 7 Cadets from Vermont who failed since no admitted Cadet was dismissed.[33]

There were many possible reasons John did not finish. However the most probable reason was John resigned his cadetship in 1838 as he was bored and had enough of the military straight-jacket. Indeed at least one obituary writer indicated as much.[34] As far as his West Point permanent

---

[31] Sherman, of course, was a Union General who led the dramatic *March to the Sea* during the Civil War.

[32] *The Best School*, page 73.

[33] Ibid. at Appendix Seven. Between 1833 and 1860, 31 Vermont residents were admitted to the Academy. Twenty-four graduated and 7 failed.

[34] *The Sun*, January 1, 1890.

record, John was deficient in mathematics, was in general a student with good study habits, but had an unmilitary propensity.[35] So John was not officer material, but by contrast even a failed or resigned West Pointer might still find himself in the enviable position of earning substantially more income serving as a superintendent of a construction project or that of a chief engineer. And that's the course John took after leaving West Point. As noted in *The Best School,* while completing the program had its rewards, it also meant a career in the army:

> The young West Pointer entering the army in the years between 1833 and 1860 probably did not concern himself very much with the contributions his alma mater was making to their growth of military professionalism. To him the pursuit of his calling meant slow promotions, frequent separations from his family, physical hardship, the drudgery of military routine, and possibly an occasional encounter with danger, all of this on a less than munificent income and no pension plan.[36]

By resigning his cadetship, John would not be involved as a senior officer in the calamitous Civil War as were his cadet mates. Instead, John would leave West Point and never look back. It was time to work on a railroad being constructed on Lake Erie.

John Hooper

---

[35] Research compiled by Robert S. Hooper.
[36] Ibid. p. 20.

CHAPTER 3

A Young Civil Engineer

A wise son <u>heareth</u> his father's instruction: but a scorner heareth not rebuke.[37]

Even though John lost his father at a young age, he had his father's aptitude for engineering. He developed additional skills at the Burr Seminary and at West Point, known as the home of the Army Corps of Engineers.

As a young engineer, John followed the work which led him to New York. John would ply his skills helping construct the "New York and Erie Rail Road." This rail road (two words in that era) was a considerable engineering feat and was charted by Governor Enos T. Thoop on April 24, 1832. There was an urgent need for this project.[38] Indeed there were

---

[37] Proverbs 13:1.

[38] imodeltrainstuff.com.

widespread concerns that southern New York "would miss out on development brought on by the Erie Canal to the north." Thus the goal "was to connect the cities and industries of this region to both the Hudson River and the fast developing shores of Lake Erie at Dunkirk."[39]

Construction commenced in 1836 and the track was built to a broad gauge (six feet) as opposed to the standard of about four feet and eight and a half inches. The hope was a smoother ride, but there was a business angle as well. As one historian noted, the larger gauge also "enabled them to carry larger items than anyone else, and only the Erie could use the line, thus keeping all other lines out of its territory."[40] The line was finished in 1851 and was approximately 446 miles long.

Where was John? He began his engineering career sometime in 1838-1839. John would have been assigned either with a surveying crew or to an engineering team. While his exact assignment is unclear, John was only in his early twenties and was earning steady income.

John probably didn't earn all those West Point demerits because of choirboy behavior. Instead, we can assume he would occasion to some enjoyable mischief and mirth. So when resting after a long day, he may have sojourned to the Lee Homestead, which was built in 1840 and used as a tavern.[41] While its heyday appears to have occurred long

---

[39] Ibid.

[40] *The Erie Railroad*, by William A. Greene.

[41] Ibid.

after John's departure, it was part of the rail road milieu during the early years of John's employment.

As with Burr Seminary, West Point, and now his engineering work on the Erie Railroad, John only had two years to go before it was time to take on the next chapter in his life. So when and why did John leave his engineering position and move back to New York City? It has been reported in one of his later obituaries that he left in 1841 to seek out a vastly different opportunity.[42] John may have been captured by a sense of destiny that pushed him to find something, somewhere that would satisfy a restless soul. Whether restless or not, John may also have had a practical reason to move on. In 1842 work on the rail road was suspended and not resumed until 1849.[43] At any rate a

A Grand Beginning

[42] *New York Times*, Dec. 23, 1889.
[43] Greene.

couple of points need to be shared about this fabulous rail road that would surely have made John proud of his role in its development.

First, and almost comically, the inaugural two-day trip occurred on May 14, 1851. President Millard Fillmore and his entire Cabinet, which included the great, aging orator Daniel Webster as Secretary of State, made the two-day journey. Webster, ever the showman and looking for one last moment of glory, reportedly viewed the scenic run from a rocking chair somehow fastened to a flatcar. It was also reported his view was enhanced with a jug of high-end Medford Rum.[44] At each stop along the way, to no one's surprise, he would summon his strength and give a stem-winding speech to the waiting crowd.

Once the festivities had concluded, and Mr. Wester was carefully detached from his flatcar seat, the business of the railroad was full steam ahead. Advertisements exploded in newspapers announcing the route and fare:

1851.
CHEAPEST AND QUICKEST ROUTE,
FROM BUFFALO TO NEW YORK.

New York and Erie Rail Road.
THROUGH IN 18 HOURS!

Baggage Checked. from Buffalo to Canandaigua, from thence direct to New York, making only one change of Baggage, and FREE OF PORTERAGE.
Passengers should secure Through Tickits at the Office of the Co. in Buffalo.
LEAVE BUFFALO by Express Train, at 8 o'clock, A. M. Through to New York in 18 hours.
Leave Buffalo by Express Train, at 5 o'clock, P. M. and arrive in New York at half past 12 o'clock the next day.
Passengers by the 9¼ A. M. Train, will take the Evening Express Train from Canandaigua, and reach New York the next noon.
Fare from Buffalo to New York.............:..$8 00.
" With 2d Class Cars from Canandaigua to New York.......................$6 75.
Passengers wishing to go by the way of Geneva and Seneca Lake, leave Buffalo by the Morning Express Train, take the Steamer BEN LODeR, at Geneva at 3 o' clock P. M., and arrive in New York the next noon.

44 Wikipedia, *Erie Railroad*.

Opening the Erie Railroad was a spectacular opportunity for a burgeoning Lake Erie region to now enjoy fast and safe transport to the Hudson. While the railroad would later have substantial financial issues, like others of the late 19th Century, for now it was marveled as both an engineering and business triumph.

Great direct route. New York & Erie R. R. ... Double tract and telegraph route. To the western and southwestern states and the Canadas ... For fares and offices see other side [New York 1857].

CHAPTER 4

Horace Greeley

The Man Who Launched John Hooper and the Country's First Advertising Agency

"Stay East young man. You are needed here."[45]

November 29, 1872, was a dismal day in New York City. Cold weather and two and a half inches of a heavy damp snow mixed with the mud and horse manure clogging the streets. The day before was Thanksgiving with temperatures ranging from 38 degrees to 27 degrees.

---

[45] Greeley didn't really say that. Just my play on his "Go west" quote.

November 29th was also the day Horace Greeley died, a man broken from a decisive national electoral defeat at the hands of President Grant, the loss of his beloved wife a month before, and the loss control of his paper, the New York Tribune.[46]

Horace Greeley and Family (Library of Congress).

Mr. Greeley's sudden passing shocked much of the nation, and it also stunned John, who had long been a stockholder (one of twenty-two) in the Tribune and at one point a Tribune board member and owner of the old Tribune Building.

---

[46] Greeley was nominated by the newly formed Liberal Republican Party (endorsed by the Democrat Party) to run for president in hopes of defeating the incumbent, President Grant. Grant won a lopsided electoral victory. Because Greeley died before the Electoral College met, Greeley's electoral votes were distributed to other candidates.

Almost certainly, John would have been part of the monumental funeral procession which wound its way through New York City, where the bells of St. Paul and Trinity churches tolled as the funeral cortege passed. Most in the lengthy volume of mourners, including President Grant and his Cabinet, did not complete the journey to Green-Wood Cemetery. Forty to fifty coaches containing the pallbearers, family and his many friends along with numerous Tribune employees did continue on. In total, the crowds that day reached fifty thousand mourners. Indeed the Tribune began its lengthy review of its founder's life as such:

THE CLOSING ARGUMENT

> Yesterday the last act in the prolonged obsequies of Horace Greeley was performed in the presence, one might say, of the whole people of the United States. In New-York and Brooklyn business came to a stand. The merchant forsook his ledger; the lawyer abandoned his books; the laborer dropped his hod; the poor girl laid aside her needle; and all stood reverently by the way side while the good gray head which all men knew was borne sorrowfully to its final rest.[47]

John, like many of Greeley's close friends, would have witnessed the opening of Greeley's vault, which only a month earlier was opened to place the remains of Greeley's beloved wife Mary. Subsequently the body of Horace Greeley "was deposited in its last resting place, and his daughters descended, and laid upon the coffin their tributes of flowers."[48]

---

[47] *New-York Tribune*, December 5, 1872.

[48]*New York Tribune*, December 5, 1872.

The Tribune paid additional respects to its great founder, noting he had gone to his grave "with the lament of the whole people; he will hold a place in their hearts as long as Americans know how to honor patriotism, unselfishness, and Christian virtue."[49]

HOOPER AND GREELEY: A LIFELONG COLLABORATION

So ended a decade-long friendship and collaboration that made them both wealthy. Indeed, Horace Greeley and John were contemporaries. Greeley was a bit younger and heralded from New Hampshire. John was a New Yorker, but also had ties to Vermont, as noted earlier. Both were members of first the Whig and then the Republican Party. They were anti-slavery. They had powerful futures ahead of them, an integral part in the newspaper business. They were young men eager to make something of themselves. And indeed they did! Both made fortunes and while Greeley rose to national fame, John played an important role of the tenor of the times.

Their relationship began around 1841 when John heard that Greeley was establishing the *New York Tribune*. John would leave a successful engineering position and start something that required no engineering and only simple mathematics. John had wandered back to his New York City home and was hungry as a capitalist and entrepreneur. John had completed his schooling and was quite finished with work on the railroad and civil engineering. John also had some newspaper experience having worked at the *Troy*

Budget, where his brother Charles Hooper had been first co-publisher (1832-1837) then publisher (1838).[50] Horace Greeley's *Tribune* would become John's life-altering opportunity, opening doors unimagined at the time. To that end, John went home to New York City to take a chance.

While eager for this opportunity, it was reported that "Mr. Greeley told him there was no opening, but Hooper said he would do whatever was assigned him at a salary of $8 a week."[51] One man who knew John indicated he began his *Tribune* career "as a canvasser,"[52] one who was not a part of the newspaper business but increased revenue by selling subscriptions and using street vendors to sell daily papers. However, John zeroed in on another revenue stream, selling print and space to advertisers. "He worked for a while, thus, and then made arrangements to bring in advertising patronage to the paper on commission."[53] Not for long.

As he continued selling *Tribune* advertising, he transitioned to placing advertisements in other papers "to accommodate a customer."[54] In no time "[o]ther papers were soon brought into the scheme."[55] It was from this rather inauspicious start that "there were grounds for considering him the oldest advertising agent in New York."[56] As noted in the *Tribune,* within "ten years he had acquired a handsome competency, but continued to develop his business until it

---

[50] Library of Congress, *The Troy Budget* (Troy, NY) 1828-1840.

[51] *The Sun*, January 1880.

[52] Rowell, p. 140.

[53] *The Sun*, January 1st, 1890.

[54] Rowell, p. 140.

[55] *The Sun*, January 1st, 1890.

[56] Rowell, p. 140.

reached large proportions and extended throughout the country."[57] Before long, *John Hooper & Company* went national. John's wandering days were over.

The *John Hooper & Company* newspaper advertising agency not only put John Hooper in the business eye, it also created an income stream that allowed his business to prosper and his personal wealth to expand exponentially. Through it all John kept it simple. Indeed, his business style was aptly described by an acquaintance, Mr George Rowell, who explained that John would place an advertisement in a newspaper and pay for it himself. He would then take the receipt to his principal and collect the funds; the transaction would be closed: no fussing with a bookkeeper and no open account. Unfortunately "a settlement in full might be delayed a little, but his customers were good."[58] Even when the bills accumulated he would still try to care for them.

John's lack of business formality seemed to bother other agents. They would say he "carried his office in his hat." As to his business style: "He was slow of speech, slow of motion; as honest as the day was long; and curiously, too, as time progressed, it was noted that he was never in any hurry about being paid, provided the customer was good and the business still being advertised."[59]

Quirkiness aside, John's style worked. His business blossomed from an "office in his hat" to a full blown advertising operation. As quaintly put by Mr. Rowell, "like

---

[57] *New York Tribune*, December 23, 1889.
[58] Rowell, p. 141.
[59] Ibid.

those farmers who find a wife cheaper than a hired girl, he took a partner instead of hiring a bookkeeper." This would not be enough. As he grew, he finally hired that bookkeeper, as well as an "estimate clerk, checkers and office boys." And since John knew the value of advertising, his company would place its own advertisements in prominent newspapers heralding the outreach of his business. Prominent, too, was his company's office location: No. 41 Park Row; New York

Advertisement in the NY Tribune February 2, 1860

Times Building. "The office was the best in the Times Building."[60]

A sampling of his own advertising suggests his prowess. Note his business territory was broad: it included the entire country.

Advertisement, The New York Times, August 29, 1860

[60] Ibid. p. 143.

And to buttress his confident approach, his company was able to advertise in both the United States and Canada. Within a matter of a decade or so, John had taken that introductory $8-a-week opportunity given to him by Horace Greeley and mushroomed it into a national concern. Newspapers were so impressed with John's business that they put their names to glowing testimonials:[61]

Commercial Bulletin, May 13, 1865

Transcription:

John Hooper's City and Country Advertising Agency, New York Times Building, No. 41 Park Row.
To Publishers of Newspapers: Gentlemen: Having determined to extend my Advertising Agency to Newspapers published outside of the City of New York, my long experience as an Advertising Agent (fifteen years), in this City will, I trust prove mutually advantageous. You will therefore oblige by extending to me the same facilities, commissions, &c., allowed to responsible advertising agents, as my bills will in all cases be paid in cash and as promptly as the
most reliable agent.
You will oblige by sending to my agency, at your earliest convenience, a copy of the paper or papers published at your office, containing the rates of advertising.
Respectfully yours,

John Hooper,
City and Country Advertising Agency, New York Times Building, No. 41
Park Row.

New York, April 15th, 1859.
To Publishers of Newspapers through the United States and Canada:
Mr. John Hooper has been in business in this city for the last fifteen years
as an Advertising Agent, during which time he has advertised largely in the
papers with which we are connected, and has on all occasions met his
payments and transacted his business promptly and satisfactorily.

Understanding that it is his wish to form a business connection with all
City and Country Newspapers as an Advertising Agent, we take pleasure in
recommending him to Publishers generally as a prompt, responsible and
efficient agent.

Horace Greeley & Co., Publishers New York Tribune
J. Watson Webb, Courier and Enquirer,
M.S. Beach, New York Sun
Francis Hall & Co., Commercial Advertiser
W. Drake Parsons, Daily News
J. & E. Brooke, New York Express
Raymond, Wesley, & Co., New York Times

Yes, John was proud of his association with Horace Greeley, whose Tribune was now New York City's largest newspaper. Evidently, Mr. Greeley was only too happy to endorse *John Hooper's City and Country Advertising Agency*. It was a synergistic relationship.

As John would soon discover, long before the *mad men* descended on Madison Avenue to ply their slick advertising schemes, his *Park Row* man success in advertising and his honest manner with his clients would pave the way for more business opportunities far different from what he had already mastered.

CHAPTER 5

I Think I'll Start a Bank

He who increases his wealth by interest and overcharge gathers it for him who is kind to the poor.[62]

Proscriptions against lending and charging interest had largely evaporated in the West by the 19th Century and before, no longer was the concern about taking advantage of someone in need of capital because of a dire circumstance. Instead banking was business and banks made loans likely to those who would repay the loan with interest.

In New York, starting a savings bank required legislative approval, a hurdle that John Hooper had been preparing to clear. By around 1865, the New York Assembly was moving certain banking legislation through the legislative process,

---

[62] Proverbs:28:8.

with the goal of incorporating the North River Savings Bank,[63] an institution that would bear John's imprint.

By January 31, 1865, the New York Assembly reported the "bill to incorporate the North River Savings Bank was ordered for a third Reading.[64] Meanwhile, on March 31, 1866, the New York State Senate reported, among other things, a bill incorporating the North River Savings Bank (In addition to a bill increasing compensation for the education of deaf mutes under 12 years of age).[65]

Eventually the politicians got out of the way, and the North River Savings Bank opened for business on December 12, 1866. The classically-inspired one-story building was located at 8th Avenue and 34th Street. John Hooper was its president.

North River Savings Bank had regular *bankers hours* of between 10 and 3 daily, but on Monday, Wednesday and Saturdays was also open evenings from 6 to 8. The bank would pay interest on deposits at 6%, "free of Government tax."[66] The bank's business hours, especially the nighttime hours, made it possible for the small deposit wage earner to bring their weekly pay to the bank at a time convenient for them: after work. While other savings banks had early

---

[63] Why North River? The Hudson River was called the North River by the Dutch, whereas the English called it the Hudson River. Gradually over time, Hudson became the standard. John Hooper's bank was located on the west side in proximity to the river. Coincidentally, another "John Hooper" (not the same man) founded a garnet mine in North River, New York, where active mining began in 1898 by which time his son, Frank Hooper, became the owner. (Perez, p. 9). —Editor

[64] *Buffalo Courier*, January 31, 1865.

[65] *The New York Times*, April 1, 1866.

[66] *The New York Times*, December 17, 1866.

evening hours on Monday and Wednesday until 7:00, North River Savings added the Saturday evening window allowing it to capture weekly earnings.

Architectural rendering of the facade of the original North River Savings Bank Building on 206-212 West 34th Street ("closest bank to Penn Station") based on an original matchbook cover. An American flag flew from a post on the roof in the center of the building. (openai.com) —Editor

As bank president, John would have been responsible for ensuring compliance with state regulations and making sure the bank remained solvent as there was no governmental safety net. John would have been the community face of the bank and would have had to manage staff and set policies. John would also have to answer to the Board of Trustees, of which he was a member. He was also the one who dealt with the occasional problem that was just interesting enough to make the daily paper. Two such problems come to mind.

It was winter and it was dark. It was also a Friday night in January, 1872, in which the bank's doors were left unlocked. Fortunately, Officer Fitzgerald was making his nightly rounds when he discovered the problem. Since he didn't have a key, our good officer most likely contacted the night sergeant who also most likely had a list of who to contact. In short order, John, after "being notified of the fact, at once visited the place, and found none of the property had been disturbed."[67] The only thing disturbed was John's Friday night with his wife and family.

There is always the need to look out for the unscrupulous fraudster. Banks collect deposits and make loans making them attractive targets for those with malicious intent. After all, they are "where the money is."[68] As John well knew, a bank can be an opportune place for a robbery or an elaborate fraud.

The fraud in this instance was a forged check in the amount of $1,000, a considerable sum in 1875. Indeed in 2024 dollars it would be approximately $28,617.[69] The caper commenced on June 22, when Arthur Johnson, alias King, alias C. White, deposited the forged check at North River using the alias C. White. The check appeared perfectly sound and was counter-signed by one Edward A. Manice and certified by the American Exchange Bank.

---

[67] *The New York Times*, January 28, 1872.

[68] FBI.gov (Willie Sutton).

[69] In 2024 dollars this is approximately $28,617 (in2013dollars.com).

With the funds on deposit, White sent his bank book to North River and drew $200.00. The money was paid, but the well-executed fraud was already starting to fall apart. After a brief investigation, it was ascertained the check was fraudulent, and word was sent to Superintendent Walling who recognized the forger was none other than a former arrestee named King. The earlier arrest had been dismissed for lack of evidence. Not this time, however.

Thinking he had successfully beguiled North River, Johnson, alias King alias White confidently arrived at the bank to draw out the remaining $800.00. While the cashier purported to pay over the balance, "Johnson was arrested by the two officers who had been waiting for him. The prisoner was taken to the Police Central Office."[70]

Caper's aside, John continued to run the bank, leveraging his successful advertising business to promote its growth. Recognizing the importance of experienced leadership, John appointed Frede E. Vulte as Secretary of the North River Bank. A respected lawyer and Under Sheriff of the County, Vulte was an excellent candidate for the role. His expertise in *writs of replevin* and similar tools made him a valuable asset to the bank, and many prominent lawyers sought his advice on complex matters.

Knowledge of this collection remedy was an essential tool for a bank attempting to ensure return of collateral upon a loan default. As North River Bank's first Secretary, "his energy

---

[70] *New York Tribune*, June 25, 1875. Chances are this scoop was delivered to the *Tribune* care of one of its shareholders, John Hooper.

and business talents soon placed that institution in a most flourishing condition."[71]

Mr. Vulte died on November, 6, 1869. As described in one newspaper he "was Secretary of the North River Savings Bank, the successful establishment of which institution was mainly due to his energy and business skill."[72]

After Mr. Vulte's death, John continued to serve as President of the bank. It also continued to thrive, but ugly rumors of a run on the bank and growing disenchantment with John by the Board of Directors threatened the bank's stability and reputation.

John Hooper

---

[71] *The New York Times*, November 8, 1869.
[72]*New York Daily Herald*, November, 7, 1869.

CHAPTER 6

"Gentlemen, What Have You Done?!"[73]

"A stone is heavy, and the sand weighty; but a fool's wrath is heavier than them both"[74]

A rumor of a run on the bank could prove disastrous for the lending institution as panicked passbook holders demand immediate return of their deposits. Almost as unsettling are rumors or stories of bank management misfeasance, or incompetence. John, the ever steady helmsman of North River for ten years had to deal with them both.

It was early October 1876. Both the *New York Times* and *The Sun* ran stories with grabbing headlines: First, in *The Sun*:

WAR IN A SAVINGS BANK

New trustees trying to eject old president

---

[73] John Hooper to the *New York Times*, October 18, 1876.
[74] Proverbs:27.

45

The rest of headline summed up the story:

A Director Declaring War to the Knife—Mr. Hooper's Letter
to the Committee—A Question for the Meeting Tomorrow
Evening [75]

The *New York Times* headline also caught the reader's eye
in a worrisome way:

Continuation of the Run on the North River Institution—
The Trustees Depose and Censure the President [76]

"Censure!" "War!" "War with a Knife!" "Continuing Run on
the Bank!"

What had the only president the bank had ever known
done to merit scandalous headlines? It depends on who you
listened to. According to opposition trustees, John had
neglected his duties and "circulated false rumors in regard to
the condition of the bank." John noted he had never taken a
salary for serving as bank president and claimed this was an
effort to eject him from his office to obtain full control.
From's John's perspective, it was a naked power grab.[77]

Delving into the stories behind the headlines, it doesn't
appear the bank run was close to calamitous. Other banks
had stepped up to ensure North River's soundness. Both news
articles referred to the run as "not large" or as a "slight run."

----

[75] *The Sun*, October 8,1876.
[76] *The New York Times*, October 10, 1876.
[77] *The Sun*, Ibid.

Yet, while *The Sun* posted a bank statement from the previous January showing total cash and investments of $817,057.64, it also reported close to $300,000 had been withdrawn since then. When asked about this withdrawal and the associated rumors, John told the *Times*:

> I have simply related the proceedings which have taken place in order to displace me; and not having confidence in men who would resort to such measures to get control of the bank, I deemed myself justified in withdrawing my money from the bank, and some of my friends hearing of this, have withdrawn theirs also."[78]

So it is fair to say, John and his friends siphoned off some $300,000 of bank value in less than ten months, with John taking the lead. In any event, the brewing battle started after John was narrowly re-elected president in January of 1876. John told *The Sun*, that "Mr. D.H. Ranney sent for me to call at his house, and told me that if I would not resign the trustees who voted against me would make war to me to the knife."

So began a fact finding committee appointed by the board to track down reports made by any trustees which had been damaging to the bank. It culminated in a scandalous resolution fully reported in the *Times*:

> Whereas, It has been referred to a Special Committee...to inquire and report concerning certain public rumors affecting the credit of the bank, which rumors were known to the Trustees to be wholly false; and

---

[78] *The New York Times*, Ibid.

Whereas, Such false rumors appear by satisfactory evidence of many persons to have been put into circulation by John Hooper, the President of the bank, while holding such office; and

Whereas, It has also appeared to such committee that during the present year said John Hooper has steadily neglected the duties of his said office as prescribed by the second by-law, namely: "To exercise general supervision over all the affairs and business of said bank, and to give his personal attendance at the bank daily, remaining there so long as necessary;" and

Whereas, Said John Hooper has not at any time been so excused, and

Whereas, It is provided by By-Law No. 19 that "all persons holding office by election from the Board of Trustees shall be liable at all times to removal for misconduct or other sufficient cause upon the vote of two-thirds of all the Trustees at a stated meeting of the board;" be it

Resolved, That said John Hooper be removed from his office of President of the North River Savings Bank, for and by reason of misconduct and other reasons above referred to, and that a copy of this resolution....be sent to said John Hooper, and also a copy sent to the superintendent of the banking department of the State at Albany.

While certainly damning enough, the following resolution was also approved:

Resolved, That the conduct of Mr. John Hooper in giving publicity, through a newspaper, on Saturday last,[79] to the dealings of the trustees of this bank with him in consequence of his misconduct while President of the bank, whereby some depositors have been induced to withdraw

---

79 *The Sun.*

their deposits, to their injury, deserves severe censure of the Trustees and depositors of this bank.

Additional reports revealed that John had previously prepared and delivered his resignation letter. It was unanimously approved by the board at the same meeting. So why did the majority trustees proceed with the harshly worded removal resolution? Was it to ensure a record of John's alleged misfeasance and to further ensure he was done for good at North River? Or just as likely, was this now public record created to humiliate John? Was this "war to the knife?"

It would appear the latter motives to humiliate and finish off John more accurately describes the unnecessary need to prepare a resolution that had been mooted by John's unanimously approved letter of resignation. John responded to the majority trustees in a lengthy "card" published in the *New York Times* on October 18, 1876. Gone was the more "business in his hat" style John had adopted early in his advertising career. Gone was any pretense of *nuance* in his writing. John was writing from wounded pride and loss of honor as one of New York's premier businessmen. He would get the last word.

John rehashed the sordid history of the past ten months. John described the process as a "radical way of getting rid of an officer legally elected" and recounted this had "created considerable astonishment in the neighborhood...."

Then John cuts to the chase. On October 9th,

49

wishing to allay the excitement which their actions had engendered and becoming satisfied that my friends and acquaintances understood the motive of the attack to be a determination on the part of a few persons to rule or ruin the bank, I resigned peremptorily and about three hours before the board met....

His resignation letter didn't affect the board. Instead these

honorable men more or less blind with spleen and malignity, without impugning my integrity or moral character, went through the farce of displacing an officer when there was none in existence to remove.

And there it was. The process had been absurd. John was more than willing to compare records with any of the opposition. John then recounted how he had advanced $2,500 from his personal funds to secure the initial building lease. He also advanced $500 of his funds towards the bank's contingent expenses. He recited his near perfect board attendance record and observed he had neglected nothing that "was essential for a president to do. Without receiving or asking any compensation whatever."

John did concede he missed meetings in "August and September last, nor have I been at the bank so often since January last, for the reason it **was not agreeable to meet scowling and plotting faces.**" (Emphasis supplied). These blunt comments were not meant for everyone, though. But he believed "from the groveling disposition of some, and the ambitious and greed of others, the deposits had been greatly reduced."

In summing up his ten years, John was a good steward of the bank he founded. Indeed the last declared dividend under John's leadership was 6% "per annum on all sums from $5 to $5,000 payable out of the net profits of the last six months, on or after Jan. 17,1876. Attested to by John Hooper, president."[80] As amply described, John's reward was a deeply stressful year for John Hooper and his family, as the knives were drawn.

So how did the bank fare after John was dispatched? Well the trustees reduced the dividend to 5% payable in January, 1878.[81] Likewise the 5% dividend was continued for January 1879.

Yet, John's bank continued on without him. By January of 1901, the bank John founded was issuing its 70th semi-annual dividend, albeit at the rate of three and a half percent per annum.[82] In December 1915 John's bank proudly declared its 100th semi-annual dividend, noting it was charted in 1866. While no longer open on Saturday evenings, the bank did keep Saturday hours, but only from 10:00 A.M. to noon.[83]

The 100th semi-annual dividend was announced from the bank's new location. That move took place in 1905. The new building was located on 31 West Thirty-fourth street, between 5th Avenue and Broadway. It was observed the "structure is at present distinctively a banking house, one

---

[80] *The New York Times*, January 9, 1876.

[81] *The New York Times*, December 28, 1877.

[82] *The New York Times*, January 09, 1901.

[83] *The New York Times*, December 28, 1915.

story high, but it has been constructed that it may be built higher...."[84]

With the expansion, the bank now had two addresses, the original on W. 34th Street and the new one on West 33rd Street, across from Pennsylvania Station. (Daily News, June 24, 1948)

John's bank later stumbled into tax preparation. As a quick observation about Benjamin Franklin's "death and

84 *The New York Times*, December 22, 1905.

taxes", the dreaded Income Tax was added to the Constitution on February 3, 1913 (the 16th Amendment). Many years later, John's bank, and a host of other Manhattan banks would provide first aid to bewildered taxpayers who had a March 15th deadline to pay at least one-fourth of their total tax. While supposedly the tax form would take only five minutes to complete, one newspaper indicated, "That's very interesting."[85]

Deputy Collector John J. Merli (left) and Collector William J. Pedrick in the new Internal Revenue Bureau office which opened yesterday. The sign says you can do your income tax return in five minutes. That's very interesting.

This seems to capture an ever vexing and continued taxpayer headache that will never change.

Other than serving as a first aid station, John's bank continued to prosper. By June, 1948, the bank had over 100,000 depositors and resources over $110 million.

Daily News, February 14, 1943

This proud announcement echoed the bank's success. Its stand-alone days were soon to end with a successful merger with The Bowery Savings Bank on February 15, 1949. The new Bowery Mutual Savings Bank boasted 500,000 depositors and over $787,000,000 in resources.[86] The bank's four convenient locations included the former North River

---

[85] *Daily News,* June 24th 1948.

[86] *Daily News,* February, 15, 1949.

Savings location. The merger was proudly announced in the

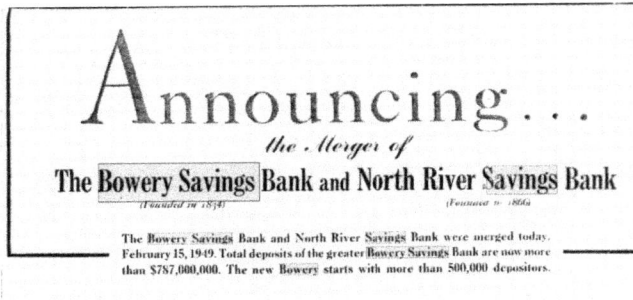

Announcing...
the Merger of
The Bowery Savings Bank and North River Savings Bank
(Founded in 1834) *(Founded in 1866)*

The Bowery Savings Bank and North River Savings Bank were merged today, February 15, 1949. Total deposits of the greater Bowery Savings Bank are now more than $787,000,000. The new Bowery starts with more than 500,000 depositors.

Daily News on February 15, 1949:

Thus two venerable savings bank institutions, the Bowery Savings Bank and North River Savings Bank became a powerful force offering substantial assets to finance the post-war boom in home construction. This is yet another lasting legacy for John, another vehicle to serve people.

John Hooper

CHAPTER 7

Lead Amassing a Fortune

He was never in any hurry about being paid.[87]

How does the founder of North River Savings Bank and an established advertiser become the leading lead manufacturer in New York? As a young adult, John may have worked at the West Point Foundry which would have introduced him to the manufacturing of armaments. He also worked as a civil engineer on the Erie Railroad project which may have given him insight on the nature of the unique lead business. Yet neither this nor banking nor advertising led him directly into lead production.

It begins with the company called Colwell, Shaw, and Williard. Colwell manufactured a patented tin-lined lead pipe. They made more than just lead pipes for the city. They

---

[87] Rowell, p. 141.

also made bullets. With several patents secured, Colwell commenced its manufacturing activity in about 1866.

To make the bullets, Colwell acquired an octagonal cast-iron shot tower that used heat, gravity, and water to make different caliber shot. The tower, located at 63 Centre Street, was about two-hundred feet tall, the equivalent of a seventeen-story building. The diameter at the base was twenty-five feet and tapered off to eleven feet at the summit. Built in 1855 by James McCullough, it was constructed of brick with ten iron pillars reaching from the foundation to the top. It was an exemplary accomplishment of advanced engineering for its time.

By 1871, Colwell Lead Company employed thirty-three men to work in the tower and adjacent buildings. They could produce up to 15 tons of shot daily.[88]

This tremendous production was not a quiet affair. A *New York Times* story published on November 13, 1881, exposed this unusual business. An intrepid reporter described the condition as he worked his way to the top of the shot tower, led by the capable superintendent, Christopher Tracy. The full headline read:

A VISIT TO A SHOT-TOWER

HOW PIG LEAD AND ARSENIC ARE CONVERTED INTO
SHINING SHOT

DROPPING MOLTEN LEAD 200 FEET—THE DEAFENING
NOISE OF A SILVERY SHOWER-DESCRIPTION OF THE
MEN AT THEIR INTERESTING WORK

---

[88] stuffnobodycaresabout.com.

The Colwell Shot Tower (nyc.gov)

"Interesting work" indeed with men wearing oven-type mitts and dealing with a deafening noise uniquely described by the adventurous *Times* reporter. As he approached the building adjacent to the tower, he noted that the clamor of sound was eardrum piercing, equivalent to one-thousand "sewing-machines in full play." As he approached the shot tower, the noise dramatically increased to ten-thousand sewing-machines.

When the superintendent opened the door the reporter was met by a gust of wind and noise "almost deafening." The reporter "was now certain that fully one-million sewing-machines were at work for all they were worth."[89]

The calamitous noise was initiated by first mixing molten pig iron with arsenic. This toxic mixture, the color of "human gore" was then dropped from the summit of the tower through one of the many sieves (different caliber sizes), with each one serving as a template for the type of shot being produced.[90] As it fell through the air it semi-cooled into a globular shape and was then captured in a twelve-foot well at the base of the tower.

Colwell Lead Company, however was more focused on lead pipe than shot, especially its patented tin-lined lead. In one advertisement (likely placed by John):

> Buy the Best—The Tin Lined Lead PIPE never corrodes by the action of water. It is cheaper than lead pipe, as it will last four times longer, and is worth nearly double as old material. It is recommended by nearly every architect in New York as "superior to all other water pipes." Be not deceived by tin-washed or tin-coated imitations. Price 16

---

[89] Mechanical sewing machines commonly used in the 1880s were noisy. The sound would be loud and distinct, with a clicking sound from the needle going through the fabric accompanied with a clattering sound from metal components interacting with each other. (openai.com)

[90] *The New York Times*, Ibid.

1/2 cents a pound. Descriptive pamphlets sent by mail free. Colwell Lead Company. 213 Centre Street

Advertisement in the New York
Daily Herald, May 3, 1874

The lead pipe was so valuable that Colwell was victimized by attempted theft of more than a thousand dollars worth of lead.[91] Showing there is nothing new, the crime was an inside job. A Colwell porter, Fred Paine, assisted the thief. After capture, the unsuccessful prisoners were held in lieu of a $1,000 bond.

With Colwell in full production, how did John get involved? John's advertising business centered on his willingness to take a risk on obtaining slow payments from a good business advertising client. John knew he would

---

[91] *The Evening World*, September, 29, 1888.

eventually get paid, except when he didn't as in the case of Colwell who was an important client. John as noted earlier was a patient man. However, this "sometimes led into assuming rather serious risks; and it came about at one period that …Colwell…had become so much in his debt that he was finally, for his own protection led to assume a proprietary interest in their enterprise."[92] So John traded debt for equity.

And that is the sum and substance of how John gained a foothold in the lead business, a business that would make him a fortune. He was already busy with his other ventures, and perhaps too busy. While serving at Colwell, John was simultaneously running his advertising business, now ensconced at the New York Times building, and serving as the president of North River Savings Bank.

With these multiple responsibilities comes the risk of over-extension, and perhaps lapses in astute decision making. It has been a New Testament standard that "no-one can serve two masters."[93] John would attempt to serve three, while also serving on the Tribune Board, and as will soon be explored sharing some of his time with his family.

It was time to reduce his responsibilities. John's advertising business included a partner named George Wayre, whose brother was E.D. Wayre, a long-time bookkeeper for George Rowell. It was perhaps a collaboration of the Wayre brothers that may have led to John's decision to part ways with his advertising agency.

---

[92] Rowell, p. 142.
[93] Matthew, 6:24.

The lead business became of so much more importance than the advertising agency that he was induced to drop the latter, and in the year 1870 I was approached with the suggestion that I buy the good will of the concern, take over such customers as could be delivered, assume the office occupied by the Hooper company, and in general succeed to the business of the oldest advertising agency in New York.[94]

In 1870, John sold "the oldest advertising agency in New York" and received a handsome price for his company's good will: $10,000.[95] He was now liberated from his tripartite responsibilities, and Mr. Rowell was satisfied with the quality of the business and noted it was the best office in the Times Building. Also, while John had moved on with his remaining ventures, he "continued to turn over small orders to us to the end of his life."[96]

John sold his advertising business, but left an interesting legacy for successor advertising agencies: the tradition of leasing space from the *New York Times*.

There is evolution in advertising offices as in everything else. The second floor of the Times building was occupied by John Hooper, the pioneering advertising agent of New York, in 1858. Geo. P. Rowell & Co. in 1870 bought out Mr. Hooper and secured possession of the desirable offices. Messrs. Rowell & Co. a few years later surrendered the offices to J.H. Bated who occupied them until the demolition of the old Times building two years hence. J.

[94] Rowell, p. 142.

[95] Approximately $241,000 in 2024 dollars (in2013dollars.com).

[96] Rowell, ibid.

Walter Thompson the well known magazine and newspaper advertising gent is the latest tenant....[97]

New York Times Building (<u>digitalcollections.nypl.org</u>)

Rendering of the Times Building

(geographicguide.com)

The Closeup View

Of course, it began with John Hooper.

While John had profitably jettisoned himself from his advertising business, he continued to hold two demanding roles: founder and president of North River Savings Bank and president of Colwell Lead Company. When he was ultimately ousted from the bank's presidency, he remained in charge at Colwell. In hindsight, given his immersion in the day-to-day demands of both ventures, the bank's board may have had reason to question his focus. Evidence suggests John had begun to let certain presidential duties lapse. Nevertheless, North River Savings continued to prosper, reflecting the strength of the institution he helped build, even as his direct engagement waned.

Now with John singularly focused on lead, with shot and pipe in full production there is yet another side story involving the shot-tower and the same Christopher Tracy who earlier led a *Times* reporter on an exploration of the shot making process. This story involved murder, just retribution, and John's shot tower.

It is fair to say that John would have been aware of both stories, especially the lethality of the latter and the newsworthy importance of what was about to happen. After all John was quite familiar with *Five Points* of New York and the desperado gangs occupying that space. Every New Yorker knew about the gangs of New York and the havoc they wreaked. The notorious *Whyos* gang was already infamous and was now about to become even more newsworthy. The gang was known for their wretched menu, a litany of harms against anyone for a price. The menu ranged from a mere "punching" of an unlucky someone for a dollar, a potentially lethal shot in the leg for twenty dollars to "doing the big job" for one-hundred dollars. Now it was time for one of the *Whyos* to pay a steep price and the shot tower would play a part in this featured story.

The intrepid reporters scoping out the Colwell shot tower and getting a scoop on the story were not from the *New York Times,* but instead *The Evening World. The World* flashed the following headline giving itself a hearty pat on the back for its news scoop:[98]

WITH THE SPEED OF THOUGHT

THE EVENING WORLD AHEAD OF ALL ITS RIVALS WITH
THE NEWS

As seen on the next page, the headline was accompanied by two sketches to help tell the story.

So what was this scoop? *Whyos* leader Daniel (Danny) Driscoll was to be hanged. The *Evening World* wanted to be "the first newspaper on the street with an account of Driscoll's execution." Seen as the paper's latest victory, the writer noted it was "achieved by a novel and ingenious method…was never before used in journalism in this city and by which not only time and space but also the steel bars and massive walls of the Tombs were overcome."[99]

---

[98] *The Evening World*, January 23, 1888.
[99] The Tombs was a city jail complex in Lower Manhattan.

What was going on at the Tombs? It was the scheduled hanging of notorious *Whyos* gang leader Daniel Driscoll for the cross-fire murder of Beezy Garrity. Driscoll had exhausted his appeals and his time was running out. While he was visited by a parish priest and two nuns, it is not clear whether he made a clean turnaround with his conscience until perhaps that fateful early morning date with the gallows. There as he walked from the prison to the enclosed yard he kissed the waiting crucifix and asked his priest to let the warden know he was sorry for his behavior.

His hanging was to take place behind the prison walls; only the reporters and other invitees would witness the execution and then thereafter make their reports. But the *Evening World* had a plan.

The scoop: The Evening World, January 23, 1888

The cast of characters for this sordid affair was also described in both print and with sketches in the same edition of the paper used to describe its triumph.

66

It was the Colwell shot tower that made the scoop possible.

In the gloom of the early morning, long before sunrise, three reporters left the office of THE EVENING WORLD. Two carried huge flags of red bunting, the poles of which were ten feet long.

The Evening World, January 23, 1888

One reporter would position himself atop a five story tenement which had a rooftop view of the gallows. With another reporter some two blocks away, along with a Colwell employee (who was also president of the American Athletic Club), positioned atop the two hundred foot tower. Now it was just a matter of waiting. First a glorious sunrise, and then the reporters in the prison yard were motioned to sit at pine tables constructed for the occasion. Finally, with Driscoll positioned on the gallows, the trap door dropped. And when it did, the Evening World reporter inside the prison yard hurriedly waved a handkerchief, to his fellow reporter positioned on top of the tenement building. This reporter in turn signaled the reporter waiting on the shot tower who then signaled the awaiting reporter housed at the Evening World building.

Justice was served. The trap door had served its purpose. Danny had paid the price. The reporters had successfully employed a clever scheme to gain a few minutes time which yielded thousands of newspaper sales. In this way, the *Evening World* scooped all the others in reporting the hanging:

> An interesting story is that which tells how THE EVENING WORLD beat its contemporaries in receiving instant news of the execution of DRISCOLL and being first on the street.
>
> Neither telegraph, telephone nor messenger service being available for the work, a series of signals was arranged....
>
> THE WORLD does not recognize obstacles, except as things to be overcome. It is bound to get there and to get there first.[100]

The World got there first because John Hooper allowed this makeshift signal corps to use the Colwell shot tower. As to why John supported this endeavor, two thoughts come to mind.

First, as noted earlier the *Whyos* under Driscoll's leadership were brutal and thought little of murdering a bystander caught in gang cross-fire. John, a prominent businessman, would have had no sympathy for Driscoll. Further the *Whyos* had been plaguing the City, and this was a bit of payback.

Second, John was fundamentally a newspaper man. His newspaper advertising company was his first major business

---

[100] *The Evening World*, January 23, 1888

success. Helping out a newspaper to get the scoop on the Driscoll execution would have been something he easily endorsed. Indeed he dispatched two employees to aid in the effort.

Colwell Lead continued to prosper solidifying John's legacy. After John died, his son became president and served for twelve years until his untimely death. By 1918 an advertisement proudly demonstrated Colwell's growth from Brooklyn to Windsor, Ontario.

John helped expand Colwell and he was handsomely rewarded for his efforts and pluck. Early on, he evidently saw promise and didn't hesitate to extend credit. This ultimately led to an exchange of debt for an equity share of the business. And the rest is history. A fortune made that would benefit many.

Colwell Lead Company (itoldya420.getarchive.net)

CHAPTER 8

The Political Man

Politics is the art of the possible
—Otto von Bismarck

John climbed the first rung or two of at least three political ladders but would far short of any Bismarckian heights, not that he ever bothered to reach that summit. So why with emerging and then continuous business success would John risk time, talent, and treasure in the political arena? The answer may lie in the tumult of the times and the growth of an emerging, and soon to become dominant Republican Party. But first John tried on the "Whig".

JOHN: WHIG PARTY ACTIVIST

John's political activities are traceable to the defunct *Whig Party* founded by Henry Clay, the then Speaker of the House. John's employer and political mentor, Horace Greeley, was an active *Whig* throughout the 1830s and 1840s. The Whigs largely arose in opposition to President Andrew Jackson in about 1833 and collapsed in 1854.[101] In the meantime it enjoyed some success, nominating and then helping elect two Whig presidents, William Garrison (who ran a *log cabin* campaign) and Zackary Taylor. Both presidents died in office and were succeeded by John Tyler and Millard Fillmore,

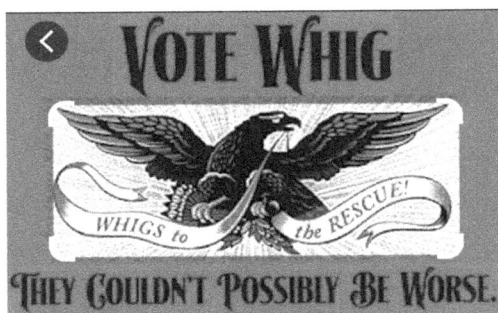

respectively. The Whigs were a fascinating group but never really formed a coherent message, other than "what have you got to lose?"

John's involvement was local and all within Manhattan's Sixth Ward, which included the notorious "Five Points"

---

[101] The name, Whig, was apparently traceable to Scottish factions opposed to curbing royal influence at Westminster.

intersection, and the area where Mother Cabrini[102] began her ministry to Italian orphans in 1889. Even in this rough and tumble arena, John would remain an active Whig for at least two years. John served as the secretary for the Sixth Ward *Democratic Whig Party*. John would attest to the three gentlemen unanimously elected to serve as delegates to nominee candidates for Supreme Court judges in their district.[103] Later, John was nominated by the Whigs as an Assistant Alderman for the Sixth Ward, Second District.[104] John would also serve as an Inspector Of Elections For the Sixth Ward, First District.

John: Republican Activist

By the 1850s, slavery was becoming a dominant and consuming issue. Both the Democrats and the Whigs had failed to stop the spread of slavery in new territories and states. The Whig Party won the presidential election in 1848, with Zackary Taylor. After Taylor died in 1850, Vice-President Millard Fillmore completed the term. This was the last Whig presidency as the party collapsed over the issue of slavery.

On March 20, 1854, the *Republican Party* was born in Ripon, Wisconsin. In 1860, its nominee, Abraham Lincoln, was elected president. The party would come to dominate the political landscape for 70 years. The party was bullish in its messaging:

---

[102] First American saint.

[103] *New York Tribune*, May 11, 1847.

[104] *New York Daily Herald*, April 8, 1848.

WE ARE COMING!

CLEAR THE TRACK!

A Political Earthquake!

THE PRAIRIES ON FIRE FOR LINCOLN!

THE BIGGEST DEMONSTRATION EVER HELD IN THE WEST!

With the collapse of the *Whig Party*, John, like Horace Greeley, gravitated towards the *Republican Party*. This point was duly noted in his favorite newspaper. As reported in the *New-York Tribune*, "[John] was a Republican in politics and several times ran for office, once for Controller of the state. He used to say laughingly that he was glad he was not elected."[105]

With President Lincoln's election, the United States engaged in a bloody, tumultuous Civil War consuming more lives than any other war before or since. John was loyal to his new party, but after the Lincoln assassination and an end to the strife, other major issues such as Reconstruction began to

[105] New-York Tribune, December 23, 1889.

ABRAHAM LINCOLN,

Library of Congress

emerge. John, like his friend Horace Greeley, may have slowly begun a departure from Mr. Lincoln's party. It was in 1872 that Horace Greeley ran for president as a "liberal Republican" only to be trounced by President Grant.

Later in 1882 John Hooper was called onto the carpet by the Party for his disloyalty. However, at least one member spoke on his behalf noting that while he was "likely to be somewhat independent upon local matters, he had voted for [the Republican ticket] when Garfield ran for president." It was later determined that Mr. Hooper would address these matters at the next meeting.[106] A meeting that may not have happened.[107]

JOHN AS A GREENBACK ACTIVIST

John would not remain a Republican. His politics later shifted as times and issues challenged this calamitous era, and as John's success grew. But his emergence as a greenback was surprising, or was it? After all the Greenback Party was also known as the *Independent Party* and it seemed John had been drifting in that direction. The Greenback Party lasted only 15 years and advocated against redemption of the hundreds of millions in non-gold backed currency (greenbacks) issued during the Civil War. The concern was that deflationary pressures would severely impact struggling famers if the greenbacks were redeemed for gold. To counter this different groups emerged, including the *Greenback Party*.

Greenback Party
(historica.fandom.com
)

---

[106] *The Brooklyn Union*, June 3, 1882.

[107] Being an independent may have meant John was also of an "Independent Movement in New York" which was "really a disaffection on the part of Republicans who are most distinguished for devotion to principles for education, social distinction, and for wealth and influence" (Eaton, D.).

By 1880, John was comfortably seated as president of Colwell Lead having parted ways with North River Savings Bank and his advertising agency. John decided to make a go for Congress by running as the Greenback candidate for Congress in the Ninth District.[108] Perhaps because John's nomination came just prior to the November election, John did not fare so well, but at least he did not finish last. Of the 28,552 ballots cast, John received a scant twenty-one votes, slightly ahead of the nineteen blank ballots cast.[109]

Despite John's dismal finish in the 1880 Congressional election, John threw his hat in the ring again in 1881. This time John ran as the Greenback candidate for Controller for the State of New York. It was reported that John "spent his means liberally in the Greenback cause. On election day he turned his house into a campaign booth."[110] The results for John were much better in his controller race, even though he fell far short of winning. John finished third with 14,878 votes far ahead of the fourth-place Prohibition ticket whose candidate mustered only 4,166 votes. [111]

The Greenback platform that John ran on had been amended at the Greenback convention in August of 1881. There was a growing confidence the Greenback Party would have good results in the fall election because they ran against "corporate abuses which they claim to have been the first to discover and wage war upon as a party."[112]

[108] *New York Times*, October 30, 1880.

[109] By contrast, other Greenback candidates received at least a percentage (greater than 1%) of ballots cast in other New York districts. wikipedia.org.

[110] *The Sun*, January 1, 1890.

[111] wikipedia.org.

[112] *The New York Times*, August 25, 1881.

Some of the more interesting resolutions included the elimination of poll taxes as a prerequisite to voting; the nationalization of telegraph companies; the granting of voting rights to all citizens regardless of sex, race or taxes; the support of the Irish in their battle against tyranny; and finally, and this was indicative of the times John lived in, the support of California's efforts to stem the tide of the "Chinese hordes".[113]

One final notable *Greenback Party* event occurred on February 22, 1882. The committee members, including John Hooper were to meet and "to stimulate united efforts among Nationals [Greenbacks] everywhere in support of all measures pending before Congress or State Legislatures which are calculated to correct the wrongs and restrain the dangerous influences of railroad, telegraph, and land monopolies."[114]

The *Greenback Party* would eventually dissolve in the late 1880s. But even with John's active Greenback Party involvement, he was also an early advocate of forming a *Metropolitan Industrial League*. The objective of this organization was protection of their interest in tariff legislation. At the inaugural meeting, "[o]n the proposition of Mr. Hooper it was decided to allow each manufacturing establishment in the City one representative in the league on payment of an annual fee of $5, and the working men of each establishment one delegate, provided their number does not exceed 100. For every 100 or fraction of 100 in excess of this

113 Ibid.
114 *The New York Times*, February 23, 1882.

number an additional delegate is to be allowed."[115] John was unanimously elected treasurer of the *Metropolitan Industrial League.*

In a follow-up, the *Metropolitan Industrial League* met at the Fifth Avenue Hotel on March 30,1882. John was in attendance and the reporter noted the league was "established in the interest of protection and is intended to antagonize the Free Trade Club".[116] And thus John was part of creating battle lines in a trade skirmish that continues to this day: *Tariff versus Free Trade.* John naturally supported tariffs not only to protect his lead business, but to ensure other manufacturers were protected from European manufacturers.

John's politics seemed to roll with the upheavals of the times in which he lived. The *Whig Party* collapsed as a result of divisions over slavery culminating in the birth of the *Republican Party* that would face the issue head-on. The travesties called the Civil War created additional horrors during Reconstruction leading to further divides along economic lines giving rise to parties such as the *Greenback Party.* John hitched a ride through this tumult and acquitted himself well remaining active into his late sixties.

---

[115] *The New York Times*, March 8, 1882.
[116] *New York Tribune*, March 31, 1882.

CHAPTER 9

Angeline Horton

A STEADY COMPASS IN JOHN'S LIFE

Shall We Ring in the New Year Together For a Lifetime?

John's steady rise to economic and civic power did not happen in a vacuum. He realized he would need a partner. While still in his early thirties, John had no idea he was starting down a path in business and politics that would become a whirlwind of constant motion. John would need a companion that would bring a sense of stability into his life. He found that steadiness when he met Angeline Louisa Horton. While Angeline was some ten years younger than John, we assume she was nonetheless well-prepared and able to take on the challenging role of Mrs. John Hooper, assisting him in his many business and political pursuits. She would also gently, if not persuasively, provide guidance on which road to travel. She was intelligent, sophisticated and well-educated. She would marry John and become a lifetime partner and counselor helping John to achieve outstanding success all the while managing their household and raising their children.

Angeline Hooper (Oil painting; artist unknown; private collection of Jacqueline Hooper)

Angeline had a true "Daughters of the American Revolution" biography. She was the daughter of John and Clarissa (Hobby) Horton, born in New York City in 1825. Both the Hobby and Horton names were steeped in colonial and Revolutionary War history. Her families were part of a colonial elite in New York and Connecticut. Indeed each surname offered (and presumable still offers) a pathway for descendants to obtain membership in various organizations, such as the Sons of the American Revolution. To add to the Revolutionary ardor, Angeline's parents were both born in 1776.

General Israel "Old Put" Putnam by Dominique Fabronius. (Library of Congress)

As to the Hobby name, legend has it that Angeline's maternal grandfather, Captain John Hobby, was housing General Israel Putnam, whose daring escape from the British has been chronicled as the "great escape" of 1779. The escape from Hobby's home is one probable version of the story, while another has the general, affectionately known as "Old Put" spotting the British while shaving in his room at Knapp's Tavern and then making a mad dash to freedom. Whichever version is correct, saving General Putnam was a great benefit to successfully winning the Revolutionary War.

As outstanding as her Hobby lineage, Angeline was also a Horton. The Horton ancestral trail leads back to William Horton who served as a Second Lieutenant of Nichelson's (sic) New York Regiment, July 1776. The following application highlights Angeline's proud Horton history:

THE EMPIRE STATE SOCIETY

OF THE

SONS OF THE AMERICAN REVOLUTION

SUPPLEMENTAL APPLICATION

Of____William S.S.Horton____, descendant of ____William Horton____

Examined and approved____December 8th, 19 3
Chas.Hall.
State Registrar.

Approved by Registrar General____1/18____1931
JBC.

I, ____William Steurer Stumpf Horton____, am a lineal descendant of____William____
Horton____, who was born in____Rye, N.Y.____

on the_____day of_____17 40 and died in____Westchester County, N.Y.____
on the_____day of_____1 , and who assisted in establishing American Independence.

I was born on the____17th____day of____March____1 862

(1) I am the son of____William White Horton____born 1856, died 1951, and
his wife ____Katherine A. V.Steurer____born 1859, died_____, married 1881

(2) grandson of____Alexander Hamilton Horton____born 1808, died 1876, and
his wife ____Margaret Larocub____born 1813, died 1883, married 1858 about

(3) great-grandson of____John Horton____born 1776 died 1814, and drowned
his wife ____Clarissa Hobby____born about 1776, died 1844, married 1803

(4) great-great-grandson of____William Horton____born 1740, died_____, and
his wife ____Ruth Heady____born_____, died_____, married 1763

(5) great-great-great-grandson of ____Joseph Horton____born 1718 died_____, and
his wife _____born_____, died_____, married_____

(6) great-great-great-great-grandson of____Joseph Horton____born 1689, died_____, and
his wife _____born_____, died_____, married_____

(7) great-great-great-great-great-grandson of____David Horton____born 1664, died_____, and
his wife ____Barnabas Joseph Horton____born 1600, died 1683, married_____

The services of my ancestor,____William Horton____(No. 4), during
the War of the Revolution were as follows:

2d Lieutenant of Nicholson's New York Regiment--July,1776.

_____

_____

Angeline's early life was most likely spent learning
subjects such as dancing, singing, and French, and assisting
her mother with the duties of the household. It is believed

84

that both of her parents were deceased by 1844 when she was in her late teens. Thus, it is possible that upon their deaths she became a teacher.

After a presumably proper courtship, she married John on December 31, 1849. While other New Yorkers were purchasing cakes for New Year's Eve tables, celebrating at a fancy ball, watching fireworks, or attending Barnum's American Museum's *Grand Gala Day* and observing the astonishing Robert Hales, the "largest man on earth,"[117] John and Angeline began their lives together. While they were nearly ten years apart in age, their marriage would blossom.[118] And John would soon discover:

> When one finds a worthy wife, her value is far beyond pearls.
>
> Her husband, entrusting his heart to her, has an unfailing prize.
>
> —Proverbs 31:10-11

Indeed, while John continued devoting time to his advertising business, Angeline cared for their home. For seven years, it was just the two of them. Did she teach during these early years of her marriage under her maiden name? Such a subterfuge was an unfortunate circumstance of the times. At one point, a regulation prohibiting marriage for teachers read:

> No woman Principal, head of department, or member of the teaching staff or supervising staff shall marry while in

---

[117] *The Evening Post*, December 31, 1849.

[118] Angeline was 24 and John was 33 at the time of their marriage.

the employ of the Board of Education, which may direct that charges be preferred against such teacher by reason of such marriage.[119]

It was not until 1904 that this regulation was set aside, but this was fifty years later and would be of no use to to the women in Angeline's society.

Was it possible that a teacher named Angeline Horton, a primary school teacher at Ward School 26, was in reality our Mrs. John Hooper incognito? An Angeline Horton was mentioned in newspaper accounts of a calamitous stampede and fatal collapse of part of the stairway that killed forty-two scholars.[120]

The day began uneventfully at Ward School 26. Divided by male and female students, and then for the little ones, into primary grades, the school day was proceeding as scheduled until about 2:30 p.m. Then Miss Abby Harrison, who was engaged with her female class suddenly became ill. She testified at the Coroner's Inquest that she felt her tongue stiffen and the muscles in her face contracted. She tried to speak and asked for the window to be opened. She testified her "appearance frightened the girls nearest to me, and they commenced screaming…"[121] What began as a scream from a number of young ladies in the rear of the school descended quickly into terror. These panicked girls burst into other classrooms instilling more horror and chaos. Of course this

---

[119] Ms Magazine.com.

[120] The term used for students during that time.

[121] *The New York Times*, November 25, 1851.

tumult aroused other students who joined the fatal stampede down the stairs breaking the newel and bannister.

It was a mere two minutes between the screams and the catastrophe, but the loss of life was immense. Of the 1841 scholars, forty-two perished on that fateful afternoon of November, 20th, 1851. The appalling casualties were broken down by department. In the primary department, twenty-two were killed out of a total of 761. When broken down by teacher, only an Angeline Horton (92 scholars) and one other were able to save all their charges.[122]

The story dominated the City papers. One summed up life's traumatic frailties as such:

> ...this city was the theatre of one of those appalling casualties, which, like lightening from a clear sky, seem to set at naught all human forecasts and prudence, and illustrate with frightful impressiveness, the uncertainty of human life.[123]

What steps this teacher took to calm her class and avoid the stampede are not clear, But since six of the eight primary teachers suffered casualties, it is safe to surmise Angeline Horton's students may have suffered losses except for her calm influence and leadership.

The tragedy was one that teacher Angeline Horton, whether or not she is our Mrs. John Hooper, would have to live with knowing she had done all she could for her 92 scholars.

---

[122] *New York Tribune*, December 2, 1851.
[123] *National Anti-Slavery Standard*, November 27, 1851.

In the same vein, beyond formal teaching, could it be our Mrs. John Hooper, using her maiden name once more, sought to advance scholarship as a "tutor or visiting governess"? An advertisement (placed by John?), appeared in the *New York Tribune*, featuring a *Miss Horton* seeking to instruct a few pupils in English, French and music.[124]

The world of Mrs. John Hooper would soon take a turn for the better with the birth of her children.

JOHN AND ANGELINE START A FAMILY

Their first child was a son born on June 30th, 1857. He was given a name common to the era—*Benjamin Franklin* Hooper (known as Franklin or Frank Hooper as attested in the 1870 Federal Census where he is listed as "Frank, a 12-year-old").

Mary Louise Hooper would soon follow in 1860. Mary's story would much later dominate the news of the day. But for now she was the precious first daughter of John and Angeline. A growing family of four, but not for long.

A mere two years later, on September 9, 1862, John and Angeline welcomed a second daughter. Like Frank, she had a rather imposing name: Henrietta Frances Hooper. She was named after her Aunt and Angeline's sister, Henrietta Francis Horton.

---

[124] *New York Tribune*, April 24, 1851.

With the arrival of Henrietta they were now a family of five. The children were born and raised in the family home located on 374 West 35th Street, 20th Ward. The mid-town residence is long gone but at the time was home to the Hooper family until at least 1885.

While the three children are listed in each census, there is precious little additional information about their formative years. However it is clear the children were educated, most likely in their home given Angeline's experience and knowledge of language and music. The children may have attended a primary Ward school, but if not it was more likely they were tutored on subjects Angeline was not comfortable with teaching.

One thing is certain, the Hooper family regularly attended Sunday services. John was Methodist and his hymnal exists to this day. The Hoopers attended Trinity Methodist Episcopal Church, Free Tabernacle.[125] The imposing edifice was located in a prime mid-Manhattan location on 34th Street only one block from the Hooper residence.

The Church had abolished "pew fees" hence the name *Free Tabernacle*. But a tithing was still important for church upkeep and its missionary extension. In the 1875 annual report of the "New York City Extension Missionary Society" the Free Tabernacle boasted substantial contributions, including all the Hoopers. John generously gave $350.00 while Angeline gave $50.00. Each of the children gave $25.00.

---

[125] *New York City Extension Missionary Society Report*, 1875.

TRINITY METHODIST EPISCOPAL CHURCH, NEW-YORK.

Sketch of Trinity Methodist Episcopal Church appearing in The National Magazine Dedicated to Literature, Art, Religion, January, 1856

It is not clear if the Hoopers continued to attend this church after it was sold in 1880. At any rate the building was later razed to make way for Penn Station. While keeping up with their religious duties, Frank and Mary each had a post primary education. Frank would attend the *College of the City of New York*, while still residing at the family home. He began his collegiate education in 1874, as member of the "Introductory Class" and completed his course of education in 1878.

Mary attended the *Normal College of the City of New York*. Founded by Thomas Hunter in 1869, the Normal College was an all-female three-year institution focusing on the liberal arts, education and science. Mary had an outstanding three years at the school and was a stellar participant in the school's Tenth Annual Commencement held on Thursday, June 26, 1879.

As reported in the New York Times and recounted in the commencement program, Mary won the coveted *Hunt Gold Medal (For Latin)*. She was also a top tier scholar with a grade point average of 93. She accomplished these academic honors and graduated at 19 years of age.

John Hooper

Program Cover
(library.hunter.cuny.edu)

HUNT GOLD MEDAL.
(For Latin.)
Miss MARY LOUISE HOOPER.

FIRST PRIZE FOR FRENCH.
Miss BERTHA WOODLEAF.

SECOND PRIZE FOR FRENCH.
($40, in Gold, given by the Pres. Board of Education.)
Miss ROSALIE HEGGL

FIRST PRIZE IN ENGLISH LITERATURE.
($40, in Gold, by a Friend of the College.)
Miss ——————————

Medal Winners. (library.hunter.cuny.edu)

CHAPTER 10

Coping with Loss

Moving Forward

Give her a reward for her labors, and let her works praise her at the city gates.

Proverbs 31:31

The 1880s were a time of financial success and political excitement for John, but also of tragedy. All seemed well when the 1880 census was enumerated. John was the proud head of the Hooper family. He was employed as a "pipe fitter", but better known as the president of a company that made lead pipe. Angeline was by his side as a wife who stayed at home. Meanwhile their son, now 22 years old was a "clerk", probably working with his father at Colwell Lead. Finally, daughters Mary, age 19, and Henrietta were listed as "unemployed", even though Mary had just been certified to be a teacher upon her graduation from Normal College, City of New York.

John finally had more time with his now adult children, especially on Sunday. After services, the family might enjoy an outing at a nearby park or visit family friends and relatives, especially cousin Mary Brackett. These were good times for a successful and seemingly happy family during that summer of 1884.

AI Composite of John Hooper and Family.
(openai.com)

With 1884 behind them, 1885 would be the year John suffered a crushing loss. With her adult children still at the family residence, Angeline died in her home on a chilly winter day. A miserable and heavy six inches of snow had fallen the day before and had turned into an unpleasant thaw. Angeline had been battling pneumonia and the cold damp weather. She finally succumbed to the illness. Her final day was Thursday, February 26, 1885. She was still young, only in her 61st year, as reported by the newspapers.

Mention of her passing was fleetingly reported in daily papers. She was the wife of John Hooper, but no mention of her children or any other aspect of her life, such as her proud Revolutionary heritage or her possible life-saving role in the calamitous stampede at Ward 26. Instead, it was sufficient to say she was married to John Hooper. Friends and family were invited to attend funeral services at her "late residence at No. 374 West 35th Street, on Sunday, March 1st at half-past 1."[126] No doubt to accommodate the completion of Sunday services.

So at the appointed time Angeline was remembered and prayed over at her funeral in the home she had "kept house" in for more than thirty years.[127] She was initially laid to rest at Cypress Gardens Cemetery.

Her untimely death was a catastrophe as it signaled the beginning of the eventual unraveling of her family. Angeline was the central figure for her children, especially her daughters. Papa, as John was probably called in the 1880s, was busy with business and politics. He was loving but absent. Mother was there every day, perhaps more than her children may have wanted or needed. But she was the one who listened to her children and knew of their dreams. That's what mothers do, so she would have thought.[128]

Understandably, her daughters in particular were devastated with the loss of Mother. Mary and Henrietta were

[126] *New York Tribune*, February 28, 1885.

[127] "Kept house" was commonly used in the census to denote the role of the wife.

[128] In a poem penned by her future daughter-in-law in 1937, called "Mother", Edith May Hooper wrote in part: "Mothers we must capture their dream And make their vision ours to redeem." Certainly Angeline would have agreed with this sentiment.

at a point in their lives when a mother would have made such a difference in their young adulthoods. Mary had graduated from school and Henrietta was only two years younger. They were steeped in the customs of their times which would have led to the indulgence of young men cautiously pursuing them. A chaperoned courtship in the late 19th-century followed a customary path that may lead to a short engagement and marriage.

But who would have chaperoned Mary and Henrietta? Their mother or perhaps their older brother. But more importantly, Angeline would have provided that needed fulcrum between young suitors and the girls' papa. Now Mary and Henrietta would go it alone and have to reckon with John. As time would ultimately reveal, this would be particularly difficult for the youngest.

And what of John? What does he do without the only real stability he had known? John was approaching seventy years and was now very alone. After Angeline's death, every turn he made at their 35th Street home was a reminder of Angeline and what he had lost. From her portrait hanging elegantly above the family hearth to the furnishings she selected and placed throughout their home. John could almost still hear her voice cajoling him to join his family for a meal or admonish him about a non-business appointment he needed to keep. Everything in their home was about Angeline and their lives together.

Perhaps to ease this pain, he left the family home behind and moved to Monroe Street in Brooklyn where he would live out his days as head of his family and as president of Colwell Lead Company.[129]

In a post-script. Angeline Hooper, (nee Horton) may have been spared the turmoil and tragedy that would follow her family in the next ten years, or perhaps if she hadn't died so young, she may have seen the turmoil coming and staved off some of the tragedies. She may have preserved her family and provided succor in times of any distress. We will never know. But for now John's family had to move on and begin a new life in Brooklyn.

---

[129] "M. B. Baer & Co. have sold for John Hooper the three-story brick dwelling, no. 374 West 34-35th street, 20.6 x 98.9 lot, for $13,000." (Lindsey, p. 784)—*Editor*

CHAPTER 11

Brooklyn without a Compass

> Better a dry crust with peace than a house full of feasting
> with strife.
>
> Proverbs 17:1

John lacked for nothing as he was a man of great means and also "an extensive owner of New York and Brooklyn real estate."[130] At one point John, as a stockholder of the Tribune and for years a Tribune trustee, actually purchased the old building before it was replaced by its current structure.

John, a practical man and well-aware of life's eventual termination, began his preparations. John purchased a large burial plot (lots 14088 through 14093) at Green-Wood for "seventeen hundred dollars."[131] Founded in 1838, Green-Wood was, and still remains a cultural and historical mainstay of Brooklyn. Green-Wood was described as being

---

[130] *New York Tribune*, December 23, 1889.

[131] Hooper, p. 114.

...permanently associated with the fame of our city as the Fifth-avenue or the Central Park....

It is the ambition of the New-Yorker to live on the Fifth-avenue, to take his airings in the Park, and to sleep with his father in Greenwood.[132]

Entrance to Green Wood Cemetery. (Library of Congress)

For John, while Green-Wood was opulent in "elaborately wrought stone, dedicated to the memory of the dead,"[133] it was also conveniently located in Brooklyn. John's purchase

---

[132] *The New York Times*, March 30, 1866.
[133] Ibid.

would ultimately become a final resting place for him and his progeny.

However, the Hooper plot would not be complete without Angeline. John arranged to move her remains to Green-Wood on November, 17, 1887.[134] It was a somber re-acquaintance with his loss only two years earlier. He had moved from Manhattan to Brooklyn and so Angeline would also move from New York to Brooklyn. From that point forward generations of John's descendants would pass through these Green-Wood gates on their way to resting with their fathers.

Getting his affairs in order didn't prevent John from remaining active in business, politics and real estate acquisitions. On November 19, 1885, John was among eighteen gentlemen who dined at Delmonico's in recognition of the business stature of Mr. Charles E. Lowe, president of the Iron Steamboat Company. While John was not yet a director of the company he was invited as a personal friend.[135]

His political activities included attendance at a meeting of *The Anti-Monopoly League*. John and a "number of well-known gentlemen" were invited "to meet in the parlors of the Metropolitan Hotel" on December, 18,1885. The "parlors were thronged with the guests of the League" who were there to discuss "the silver question in its relations to the finances and commercial needs of the country."[136] The silver question

---

[134] green-wood.com.

[135] *The Sun*, November 20, 1885.

[136] *The Sun*, December 17, 1885.

would have been much aligned with John's involvement in the Greenback Party.

As to John's business interests, he was elected to the board of directors of the Iron Steamboat Company at the board's annual meeting on November 3, 1886. That company had only been in existence for five years and initially provided service to only Coney Island before expanding to other nearby locations. The fleet first consisted of seven iron-hulled steamboats named after constellations such as *Pegasus* or *Perseus*. As John expanded his business interests to now include steamers, it was time to try one out, and perhaps keep parental control over his daughters.

TIME FOR A HOLIDAY

Brooklyn in mid-July and August? One New York City poet and John's future granddaughter summed it up well:

Enough of hot breath,
And red cheeks of fever,
Take temperature of sick-
A-bed, that days don't turn over—
Heat so thick.
And worse off
Open windows that will not cool off.[137]

—Grace Duncan Hooper

---

[137] From "Citified" found in *Finding Grace, Meandering Through the Life and Writings of Grace Duncan Hooper*, pp. 105-106 (Available at amazon.com).

So how to escape the unyielding City heat? An excursion along the Hudson River and a month or so at Saratoga Springs was the perfect tonic to escape the dogs days of summer. And that's what John with his daughters in tow endeavored to do.

As widely reported, John and family summered at the Kensington Hotel until September 1, 1887.[138] The Kensington at Saratoga Springs was a dream getaway for weary New Yorkers. Saratoga Springs had a well deserved reputation as the "Queen of the Spas", but was more than just a place for haleness, it was also a horse-racing and gambling Mecca.

To get there, the Hoopers booked a steamer from Brooklyn and traversed the Hudson on a day trip to their destination. If the Hoopers traveled on the *Day Line* they would have enjoyed restaurants and writing rooms, a band, and for John a chance to get a haircut.

Perhaps John saw this Hudson excursion as an opportunity to retrace some of the steps on his multi-detoured life travels as the Hudson River trip included a brief visit of West Point, his home for two years. His daughters would have also enjoyed the fantastic views as their steamer pushed up the Hudson to Albany.

Upon disembarkation from their steamer, John and company would then travel the short distance to Saratoga Springs latest luxury, the Kensington Hotel.

---

[138] *The New York Times*, July 26, 1887; and *The Brooklyn Daily Eagle*, July 17, 1887.

Hudson River Day Line. (Library of Congress)

Kensington Hotel-The Hooper's Home For Summer Holiday. (Library of Congress)

The hotel featured rich carpeting in the common areas and was well-lit. Large stairways and an elevator to reach the upper floors were featured.

Once finally ensconced in their guest chambers, John's daughters may have marveled at the view from their balcony as their room would have undoubtedly faced either Union or Regent Street. The opulently appointed rooms were complete with indoor plumbing.

While the Kensington was the Hoopers' plush summer home, Saratoga Springs was their destination. It offered numerous amenities. Of course the "Saratoga Race Course attracted those with money to spend frivolously....Following an afternoon at the race track, millionaires gathered to gamble for high stakes surrounded by high Victorian elegance." [139] This was after all the "gilded age" where great wealth and extravagance went hand in hand.

This was the summertime idyll craved by big city denizens longing for the fresh and healthy springs of Saratoga. In addition to the spas, the activities included "hot air balloon ascensions, hops, balls...and afternoon carriage promenades down Broadway where people and horses were adorned in the latest finery." [140] There were lake excursions with fine dining at a lakeside restaurant. Many business deals were cultivated and consummated during afternoon meetings on the "wide porch on the huge hotels."[141] No doubt after a day at the races, John was making deals on the front porch.

---

[139] www.discoversaratoga.org.

[140] Ibid.

[141] Ibid.

*Race Day! Illustration (Samantha at
Saratoga, Marietta Holley, published 1887)*

This was the last publicized summer holiday for John and his daughters. While still under their father's watchful eye, they had a summer to remember, lasting six weeks before their return back to Brooklyn on September 1st. Perhaps the trip had not gone as well as John had expected, because he proceeded to execute his first will, one that would lead to both rebellion and acquiescence. But first their brother was about to get married. It would be an "all Colwell" wedding.

FROM COLWELL LEAD TO DIAMONDS

Profits from lead must have attracted diamonds, in this case uniting two Colwell Lead Company families. The Hoopers were well established at Colwell. John was president and his son, Franklin was being groomed as successor. Alva Stone Walker, a newcomer into the Hooper lives, would make a profound generational impact, beyond merely his last name.

Alva Stone Walker was born in 1836 and died in 1911. In between these milestones, Alva lost his wife Emily in 1876 and took his young family from Indianapolis to New York City. One of his children was Edith May Walker. She was born on May 14, 1867. Alva moved to New York City because there was work to be done building hotels. And that's what he did. He also purchased at least one along the way,[142] located on 81st Street in Manhattan, which was a residential hotel—a popular establishment at that time.

As to hotel construction, he built the elegant Hotel Beresford. "The structure was built by Alva Walker in two phases."[143] The second phase was completed in 1892 with the dining room moved to the top floor. It was from this dining room kitchen where meals were prepared for Alva's daughter, Grace, who was known to throw "Champagne and lobster parties all night long in her suite at the Hotel Beresford."[144]

Alva became vice-president of Colwell Lead, and it was perhaps this fortuitous circumstance that brought the young clerk, B. Franklin Hooper and Alva's daughter, Edith May Walker, together. The young couple began a courtship culminating in a proposal of marriage.

---

[142] As reported in *The Sun*, Alva Stone Walker sold the Hotel Winthrop, a six-story brick building, for a princely sum of $300,000. This occurred on about January 18, 1892.

[143] Wikipedia.org

[144] Hooper, p. 59

The engagement was announced on November 28, 1887, in the *New-York Tribune*. Franklin and Edith were married on June 14, 1888, in what the *New York Times* called "[o]ne of the largest and most fashionable weddings of the season."[145] And as reported in another paper, the "[c]ards are out for the wedding of Miss Edith May Walker, daughter of Alva S. Walker to Benjamin Franklin Hooper."[146]

The weather for that Thursday afternoon wedding was fair, and the setting was at the magnificent *Church of the Puritans,*[147] which was regularly attended by the Walker family.

CHURCH OF THE PURITANS, PRESBYTERIAN, 15 WEST 130TH STREET.

---

[145] *New York Times*, June 15, 1888.

[146] *New York Tribune*, June 11, 1888.

[147] This church, dedicated on April 15, 1875, is still standing today.

*Membership Lists from The Church of the Puritans,
Presbyterian: 130th Street, near 5th Avenue New-York (1889)*

The wedding ceremony was officiated by the Reverend Dr. Edward Clark who was assisted by Reverend Dr. James M. Dickson. The *New York Times* wedding reporter dispatched to attend and report on the event was exuberant in describing the bride's attire:

> The bride was attired in a most becoming gown of white faille Francaise[148], cut train and trimmed with exquisite point lace. Her veil was of tulle. The only jewelry she wore was a diamond pendant, the gift of the groom. She carried a bouquet of white roses and lilies of the valley.

Edith May was accompanied by her sister, Grace Walker, as her maid of honor. One of her bridesmaid's was the groom's

---

[148] Francaise faille is a French fabric with a ribbed or corded texture. Tulle is a lightweight, net-like fabric often used in wedding veils.

youngest sister, Henrietta Hooper. The bridesmaids wore "directory gowns of white crêpe de chine with golden embroidered girdles. They carried huge bouquets of la France roses, tied with pink satin ribbons.[149]"

As for the groom, little is said—it's not really his day. The story did provide the names of the best man, R.E. Carey, and four ushers: the bride's brother, Fred, L.A. Knevals, P. I. Mills, and William Buhler, Jr.

Finally, the reception was held at the residence of the bride's parents, 157 West One Hundred and Twenty-second-Street.

With the wedding behind them, John would soldier on as a Brooklynite, remaining occupied in business and organizing his affairs. Clearly he had acquired enough wealth to satisfy many legatees. But it was likely that his daughters might have occupied much of John's time. This was a possible reason he had taken a holiday with them to Saratoga Springs. Could a desire for emancipation and the right to a lasting romantic relationship with a man of their choice be a likely cause? Wanting emancipation and achieving it would prove to be difficult and costly. The young maidens were weighed down by their father's restrictions and demands.[150] Oh, how they were missing their mother.

---

[149] The groom's other sister, Mary Louise, was not party of the bridal party suggesting a possible growing friction in the family, although her absence could have been due to myriad causes.

[150] As marriageable young women of high society, they would be severely restricted not just by their father's wishes but even more so by the customs and expectations of their peers and other families of their rank.

CHAPTER 12

Willful or heartbroken?

A LOVING FATHER OR KEEPING CONTROL?

In the name of God, Amen

This was the first sentence of John's *Last Will and Testament*, which when finally probated would begin an engaging and national headline-grabbing saga and conversation. But first certain steps need retracing before the calamitous reading of this document.

New Year's Day, 1889. John's last New Year's celebration. As the New Year awakened, John was still listed in *Lain's Brooklyn Directory* as a manufacturer living at 281 Monroe Street.[151]

As to the New Year, at least one newspaper noted the significance of the day:

> New Year's Day has been regarded as an occasion of peculiar significance from very early ages. The fact that it marked the closing of an old account with time and the opening of a new one caused it to be regarded by the ancient Romans as a peculiarly fitting time for the reconciliation of differences, the making of good resolutions, the exchanging of visits and the giving of *strenae,* or presents, to relatives and friends.[152]

Almost like New Year's Day clockwork, another news story featured the foolishness of Messrs. Giggles and Wiggles and the possible delight they brought to many maidens on New Year's Day.[153] They would ring the doorbell and give out a hearty "Happy New Year!" As Mr. Wiggles and Mr. Giggles walked down the stoop, they were identified respectively as the accomplished perfume counter clerk, and the cashier. "These young men were the admiration of a large circle of young ladies. If there was anybody in Brooklyn more dignified than Mr. Wiggles those young ladies would have liked to know it; that there was anybody more witty than Mr. Giggles was impossible for them to conceive."[154]

And with continued mirth and merriment the Wiggles and Giggles saga continued much to the delight of the paper's readership, including, perhaps at least one of the young maidens living with her father on Monroe Street.

---

[152] *Times Union*, December 28, 1889.

[153] *The Brooklyn Eagle*, January 2, 1889.

[154] Ibid.

But just a week later, the foolishness of Wiggles and Giggles was swept away by the *Brooklyn Tornado of 1889*, a wintertime tornado which cast an early pall on the New Year. Not only was this weather event exceedingly rare, the *Brooklyn Eagle* headlined the event like the "EXTRA" it truly was:

FIRE AND WIND

South Brooklyn Treated to a Brilliant Display.

Why some of the Residents of That Section of the city Thought that the End of the World Had Come—The Ravages of the Tornado—Blazing gas and Shattered Tanks —The Navy Yard Barracks Decapitated—A Memorable Night[155]

Indeed it was memorable and ghastly frightening when the huge gas tank at Citizens' Gas Light Company exploded as a result of the storm's ferocity. As was reported, "[I]t was accompanied with the noise and all the terrifying effects of a wild Western tornado...."[156]

The wild west weather quickly dissipated and Brooklyn returned to its normal East Coast weather patterns.

Meanwhile, John was not slowing down. He continued as president of Colwell Lead Company and owned much of the stock. His son was listed as a clerk and Alva Walker was still vice president.

---

[155] *The Brooklyn Eagle*, January 10, 1889.
[156] *The Sun*, January 10, 1889.

Beyond lead, or perhaps because of his success there, John's business influence continued to expand when he was named a board director of *The Anglo-American Electric Light Manufacturing Company*.

What did this company manufacture?

> [S]torage batteries or accumulators, [rechargeable batteries] which are acknowledged by experts to be far superior to any other now known to the scientific world.
>
> [A] number of contracts have already been made and executed for subsidiary companies showing a handsome dividend already earned upon the capital stock, and, according to the terms of such contracts, guaranteeing a large and profitable legitimate manufacturing business...[157]

Thus to keep up with the growing consumer appetites of Anglo-Americans, there was an immediate need to increase manufacturing and as such a limited number of shares were offered at $5.00 a share to raise capital for that expansion.

Separately, John was still acquiring real estate. He purchased a two-and-a-half story brownstone for $8,000. The structure measured twenty by forty-five and was located at 829 Marcy Avenue in Brooklyn. The new acquisition was only a short walking distance from John's Monroe residence— ideal for his growing real estate portfolio. He also purchased one each at 524 and 526 Pearl Street respectively (again close to his Monroe residence) for $25,100 from a "referee", presumably a bankruptcy case.

---

[157] *The New York Times*, April 25, 1889 (Prospectus appearing under "Financial").

John expanded his charitable empire. Perhaps he knew he couldn't outrun Father Time, and realized he still had an opportunity and energy to focus on the least of New Yorkers, especially children.

One such charity was the *Brooklyn Society for the Prevention of Cruelty to Children*. This critical organization was chartered by the State of New York in 1880 and began operations in 1881. Funded by charitable giving, the Society cared for children abandoned, abused, or exploited for child labor. The Society sheltered children, organized placements in foster care, and endeavored to keep the children in school. Medical treatment was also provided.

The Society was but one of many which stepped up during these opulent times to render life-saving aid and comfort to the numerous children left in the wake of the push for industrialization. For instance, the *Little Mothers Aid Association* was founded in 1890, with the help of another Hooper, Mrs. B.F. Hooper, John's daughter-in-law.[158] Likewise, Mother Cabrini and her sisters arrived in 1889 to administer to Italian orphans. The needs of those times seemed endless.

John, along with other prominent Brooklynites, was elected to the Society's board on February, 26, 1889. It was a job he presumably was eager to undertake and as was later shown, he offered both his time and treasure to the Society in addition to many others.

---

[158] Hooper, R. J. *Born to Responsibility.*

Amidst these charitable activities, at home he still had to navigate his relationships with his daughters. There were significant disagreements between them in November of 1887 and would be revisited again in March 1889. This was the month he became grandfather to Emily May Hooper, born to Franklin and Edith May on March 21, 1889. Despite this new familial role as grandfather, John continued to maintain a harsh position regarding his daughters.

John Hooper-Original Photo Late 1880s

Edith May (nee Walker) Hooper with baby

"Papa, Please Understand"

Were these the gentle words uttered constantly by John's daughters, especially Henrietta? Henrietta was not yet twenty-four years old when her mother died, and no longer had her guidance when it came to affairs of the heart. Her sister, Mary, was less than three years older and was similarly in need of direction. Their older brother was likely sympathetic but busy with career and his engagement to Edith May Walker.

Henrietta and Mary were saddled with living in the Gilded Age while dealing with Victorian expectations. These expectations included a father's permission to move forward with a relationship that may culminate in an engagement and eventual marriage. Evidently, John was not going to budge. A detailed story was published with the following headline:

He was cranky on marriage[159]

And yes, he was was cast unsympathetically as an old man with many "unreasonable prejudices…His most senseless hobby was his extreme unwillingness that his daughters should get married."[160]

Up against this formidable foe, Henrietta still tried to "indulge the tender passion." She had found her young man three or so years prior to John's passing. That is about a year after her mother had died. As reported: "Henrietta accepted

---

[159] *The Salt Lake Herald*, dated January 2, 1890.
[160] Ibid.

the attentions of a young man who would have made undoubtedly an excellent husband. The young man wanted Miss Hooper to marry him, and Miss Hooper in fact had about accepted him."[161] By these accounts, she fought hard to get her father to accept the courtship. But the months went by and he remained disagreeable and stubborn to her wishes.

Mary also joined in the courtship fray. She was twenty-seven years-old and had fallen "in love with Dr. John A. Steurer, a doctor living at 78 West Forty-seventh street in this city."[162] Dr. Steurer was born in 1852 and had graduated in 1873 from the Bellevue Hospital Medical College. He served as an intern at the Bellevue complex and also studied abroad for two years. He started his New York practice in 1876 and was a man of means and presumably was not courting Mary to obtain a chance at the family fortune. Dr. Steurer was also described as one with "excellent habits, thoroughly respectable, and with a large and growing practice."

Dr. John Steurer was a familiar figure to the Hoopers; his younger sister, Katherine, married Angeline's beloved nephew, William White Horton (the son of her brother, Alexander H. Horton) eight years prior.[163] Despite all of this, John Hooper remained unmoved.

John's refusal to allow his daughters' courtships to blossom into marriage was perhaps a good reason to embark on the six-week trip to Saratoga Springs in 1887. It may have been a last ditch effort by John to cool the fever of his young

---

[161] *The Courier-Journal*: Louisville, January 11, 1890.

[162] Ibid.

[163] Katie Steuer NYC Marriage Records: 1829-1938; myheritage.com.

daughters' requited love for their young suitors. A change of scenery coupled with an opulent vacation may have been John's way of signaling to his daughters that this was a style of living they had become accustomed to. The girls were surrounded by the trappings of the moneyed class which they could keep if they obeyed their father. But just beyond the veneer of great wealth was a City with immense poverty. Oh how lucky to be the daughter of John Hooper, one would have thought, and steer clear of the rabbling middle and under classes.

But the memories of Saratoga Springs were perhaps short-lived. John and his daughters were back in Brooklyn in early September, 1887. John had his business empire to manage and was still dabbling in politics. Unfortunately for John, his daughters were back with their suitors. A scant two months later, John acted with conviction.

On November 16, 1887 John executed his *Last Will and Testament*, spelling out his displeasure plainly and unmistakably. He would essentially disinherit Mary and Henrietta. Each would receive "the sum of $500 only."[164] While not an insignificant sum, it was a paltry inheritance when compared to their papa's $5 million estate.

In effect, John apparently signaled to his daughters:

> Continue with your irresponsible disobedience and you will receive less than one-tenth of a percent of the estimated five-million dollar estate.

---

[164] *The Last Will & Testament of John Hooper.*

It was up to each of his daughters to decide which path to travel. His Will was more than just his last testament, it was his last word on the subject of courtship and marriage. Stay on the current path and you are disinherited and possibly impoverished. While their brother was the busy suitor of young Edith Walker with his father's blessings and eventually much of his fortune, the girls were left with an imponderable decision.

By several accounts, Henrietta bravely continued for a time with her courtship knowing she risked potential disinheritance if her father didn't soften and amend his will. She was in love but eventually she had to let him go. Her only life had been one of majestic plenty, living during the heights of the Gilded Age. Would Henrietta risk this for love? She couldn't do it. She would work her way back into her father's graces.[165]

Mary, stubborn to the end, refused to give up her relationship with Dr. Steurer. And perhaps she had a better hand to play than her younger sister. As her cousin's-in-law brother, Dr. Steurer already had a successful practice to cushion against the loss of her inheritance.

With trepidation, "Miss Mary walked out of the house one day, met Dr. Steurer, accompanied him to the home of the Rev. Dr. G.F. Krotel, pastor of the Lutheran Church of the Holy Trinity in this city, and was there married." That particular day happened to be March 3, 1889, her 29th birthday.

---

[165] One paper retracted its story that Henrietta had separated from her husband to gain her father's favor. In fact she had never married. New York Tribune, January 3, 1890.

She made no secret of her intent, and shortly before the marriage her father went to his lawyer, Treadwell Cleveland, and made a [new] will."[166]

Once again, it is possible that John had seen enough. Mary was now married. Was she hopeless and ungrateful? Was Henrietta, still at home, contrite? John made a second will, revoking the first and, when published upon his death, made headlines from New York to Seattle. Many were sensationalized to extract newspaper sales. The Sun's New Year's Day headline read:

DISINHERITED HIS GIRLS

WILLFUL JOHN HOOPER SAID HIS DAUGHTERS
SHOULDN'T MARRY[167]

Another headline zeroed in on John's "recalcitrant" daughter Mary Louise:

A MILLIONAIRE'S CHILD

DISINHERITED BECAUSE SHE MARRIED AGAINST
HIS WISHES[168]

John Hooper Makes His Son Rich and Gives $75,000 to
Charity But Cuts Off One Daughter

With a Small Income and Gives the Other $500.[169]

---

[166] *The Sun*, January 1, 1890.

[167] Ibid.

[168] *Times Union*, December 31, 1889.

[169] The identical headline appeared in *The Brooklyn Daily Times*, December 31, 1889.

And then a headline that seemed to look with enmity at the legacy of the founder of America's first advertising agency:

John Hooper's wrath

He nurses it up to the day of his death[170]

And a story of John's passing appeared *The Courier-Journal*, out of Louisville, Kentucky with a now familiar refrain:

DISINHERITED HIS GIRLS

A NEW YORKER FORBIDS HIS GIRLS TO MARRY AND PRACTICALLY DISINHERITS BOTH THE OBEDIENT AND DISOBEDIENT[171]

The *Irish Standard,* wryly observed,"[e]vidently the old saying, 'charity begins at home', did not go very far with old John."[172] Finally a Seattle paper, *The Post-Intelligencer*, summarized the scandal and then observed that while the Will will not be contested. "…all the same, it ought to be."[173]

Fortunately there were benevolent headlines such as

Mr. John Hooper dead

---

[170] *The Brooklyn Citizen*, December 31, 1889.

[171] *The Courier-Journal,* Louisville, Saturday Morning, January 11, 1890.

[172] *The Irish Standard*, January 25, 1890.

[173] *The Post-Intelligencer*, January 27, 1890.

Heart disease carries off the founder of America's first
advertising agency[174]

This gently written obituary highlighting John's business and political career, was published only a day after John's death and before the will was probated and made public.

Another headline started on the positive:

John Hooper's will

He leaves a large bequest to charity[175]

Yet even with this sanguine headline, this promising start to the story couldn't ignore the elephant in the room. It had to include that "one of his daughters, the wife of Dr. John A. Steurer, is wholly disinherited for marrying against his desire, and another, who abandoned her *objectionable swain*, gets $20,000."[176] The casual reader of that time would have been aware that *swain* was slang for a male lover or admirer.[177] The objection was of course all John's and not Henrietta's. Yet the story and others made clear her choice was grounded in holding onto the wealth she had known, a point John elaborated on in his will.

What John had to say was more than just a reference as to why Mary was left out of the money and Henrietta was back in his graces. Instead it was a lengthy and spirited defense of the decisions he made. To begin with he spells out the distinctions:

---

[174] *Brooklyn Eagle*, December 23, 1889.

[175] *Brooklyn Eagle*, December 30, 1889.

[176] *Ibid.*

[177] dictionary.com.

SECOND: To my daughter, Mary L. Hooper, I give and
bequeath the sum of five hundred dollars.

THIRD: I give and bequeath to my Trustee hereinafter
named the sum of twenty thousand dollars....[t]o collect
the rents issues, income snd profits thence arising and to
pay over the same semiannually unto my daughter
Henrietta F. Hooper during the term of her natural life....[178]

So there it was, Henrietta was rewarded and Mary disinherited. John did try to explain his thinking later. In what was most likely a verbatim recitation of his thought process was set forth in paragraph 29:

On the sixteenth day of November Eighteen Hundred and
eighty seven, I made a previous Will in which owing to the
unsatisfactory conduct at that time of my daughter Mary L.
Hooper and of my daughter Henrietta F. Hooper, I gave and
bequeathed to each of them the sum of Five hundred
dollars only[.] In that instrument I stated the reasons why I
had left to each of my said children so small a legacy. Since
that time my daughter Henrietta F. Hooper having evinced
a desire too comply with my wishes and advise, and having
given up the purpose which she then had in view, I have
revoked the [November Will]...made for my daughter
Henrietta F. Hooper the provision hereinbefore set forth.
The reasons which induced me in [November 1887], to
take the course I did, in relation to my daughter Mary L.
Hooper, and which I adopted after due deliberation had
thereof were the following:

I have for some years past earnestly and faithfully as her
father advised and endeavored to persuade my daughter
Mary L. Hooper not to engage herself in marriage or to

---

[178] At least John would not govern Henrietta"s life and choices from the grave. His will
provided that upon Henrietta's death the trust principal would be divided between and
among her lineal descendants. (But of course not to any husband! Simply to her chidden.)

marry the person who was then paying his addresses to her: my advice apparently produced no effect upon my said daughter Mary L. Hooper: she condemned and defied my advice in this matter and repeatedly disregarded my wishes and disobeyed my commands, and believing that the said person was not a person whom she should marry, I deliberately and after due reflection and great reluctance determined to give my said daughter no other portion of the estate other than the sum of Five hundred dollars, since [November 1887] I have continued to advise my daughter as before but she has continued the same willful course and in causing me the greatest distress. I therefor as to her adhere to my former purpose....

John's "former purpose" was to disinherit Mary. While Henrietta fared much better, she would never have control over her legacy since it would be managed through a trust. She would receive only the income from that trust. Her descendants, if any, would receive what was left in the trust.

While John's generosity was sprinkled throughout his will, it was paragraph 29, that stirred things up and helped newspapers sell more copies than they would have during the holidays of 1889-1890. It was ironically John's final gift to the papers he had generated so much of his income as New York's first advertiser.

Yet despite the headline-grabbing story of disinheritance, Mary remained defiant. She had already married Dr. Steurer in a Lutheran service before her father died. And after John's passing when Mary and Henrietta had to indulge the indignity of scandalous headlines, she was confronted by a reporter on New Year's Eve, 1889. She was with her husband and her brother, at her new home. She stated that

> Father was a monomaniac on some subjects…and among these was this one of us girls marrying. He was about crazy when it was ever talked of, and he was just so when any young man would come to the house. If a young fellow would come once in two weeks father would say: "What? Is that fellow here again."

> I had to choose between love and money, and I chose the former. I don't think there will be any contest of the will.[179]

The estate's big winner, brother Franklin, agreed their father was unreasonable about a good many things. He indicated he was on amicable terms with both sisters and thought (hoped) a will contest would be unlikely. And of course he was correct. Mary had little chance of successfully challenging her father's will. Absent a showing of undue influence or incompetence, she would not prevail. Likewise, Henrietta, who had at least been provided lifetime income from a trust created by her father's will, would have no incentive or strength to mount a challenge.

And so the question remains, was John acting out of willful spite or was he heartbroken? His treatment of Mary and Henrietta seemed harsh and unrelenting. If Dr. Steurer could not gain favor with John, who could? It seemed John was intent on ruining any chance for his daughters to pursue happiness in romantic relationships unless they were willing to forfeit their inheritances.

Yet before John is cast as a miserly, spiteful father, the depth of his heart was also filled with charity to many,

---

179 *The Sun*, January 1, 1890.

including critically important charities caring for the poorest and most wretched living just outside the growing wealth and power of New York City. It seems the question of John's heart needs further exploration.

John Hooper

CHAPTER 13

He was a Good Uncle

AND REMEMBERED MORE DISTANT RELATIONS

Even by his neighbor the poor man is hated, but the friends of the rich are many. [180]

John's beneficiaries extended well beyond his Brooklyn confines and his non-lineal descendants. John had amassed a fortune and drizzled out his bequests as outlined in several paragraphs of his will. He did this while deliberately impoverishing one of his daughters and leaving the other at the mercies of her trustees. What might have been even more galling to his daughters was the sums he bestowed on his nephews and nieces, all first cousins to Mary and Henrietta.

First, John awarded six-thousand dollars to each of his nieces, all of whom were his brother Thomas Hooper's daughters. They were Emma E. Hooper, Jessica M. Hooper, Claudia F. Johnson, wife of Frederick W. Johnson, Clarinda A. Underhill widow of Henry L. Underhill and Laura H.D. Hooper.

John's brother Thomas and his wife, Emmeline, resided in Brooklyn. At the time of John's death, Thomas was manufacturing *looking glasses* or ornate mirrors. It cannot be understated that John's generosity to his nieces provided a substantial benefit to his brother as well. At the time of the 1880 census all his daughters, including Clarinda Underhill (widow), were living at the family home along with Clarinda's two sons. By 1900 Thomas was an 87-year-old widower, still working as an artist. As to his home situation, not much had changed as four daughters remained at home, while only Claudia had left the family home after marrying Frederick Johnson.[181]

John's nephews Charles B. Hooper and Charles T. Hooper were given life estates for the properties located at 285 Monroe Street and 289 Monroe Street, respectively. Upon Charles B. Hooper's death the property would descend to his heirs. But, John was more restrictive with who should receive the property after Charles T. Hooper died. Only the lineal descendants of his second wife, Mary Jane Hooper would receive the property.

Who were these nephews, both named Charles, and why were they granted a real property interest in Monroe Street

---

[181] For whatever reason John neglected to provide his brother's son with any inheritance. His son Thomas was still living at home and was employed as a "salesman".

property? It appears his nephew Charles T. Hooper was the son of William Hooper, John's older brother. Tragically, William died in 1833 at the age of 29. He died the same year his son Charles T. Hooper was born. Charles was thus born without a father in his life. It is entirely probable that John, while busy with his own life, kept a watchful eye on the son of his deceased brother. After all, John had also lost his father at a young age.

Charles T. Hooper (private collection)

By the time of the 1855 Census (New York), Charles T. Hooper was married to Juliet (Wellslager) Hooper and had an infant child, Ella. He was employed as a gilder.[182] By 1860, Charles T. Hooper was designing picture frames. He was still married to Juliet and now had two children. In 1868, Juliet died.

---

[182] Someone who applies gold or gilt as an ornamental overlay.

Eight years later, on February 8, 1876, Charles T. Hooper married Mary Jane Taylor. At that time, he had his own business and may have been in employed with his uncle Thomas Hooper.

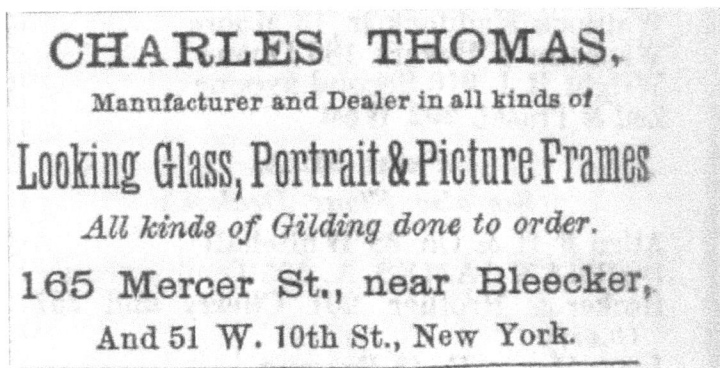

CHARLES THOMAS,
Manufacturer and Dealer in all kinds of

Looking Glass, Portrait & Picture Frames
All kinds of Gilding done to order.

165 Mercer St., near Bleecker,
And 51 W. 10th St., New York.

Advertisement in the Building Business Directory of New York, 1871-1872

Both Thomas and Charles were listed in the same business directory and both had an occupation of making *looking glasses*. As such it appears they worked at the same business location.

And then there was the other Charles, Charles B. Hooper. Like his cousin, this Charles also received a life estate on Monroe Street, with his heirs receiving the property. Charles B. Hooper was born in 1838 in Troy, New York. Charles was a bookkeeper and was married to Emaline. At the time of the 1880 Census, Charles and family were living on 281 Monroe Street in Brooklyn, not far from his future inheritance located at 285 Monroe Street. It also appears Charles may have been a bookkeeper employed at Colwell Lead Company.

Other interesting legatees included Annette Ferris of Lamartine, Wisconsin who received $6,000 and Amelia Redfield, of Winona, Minnesota who received the property at 287 Monroe Street for her life. Upon her death the property would go to her heirs. And finally, John bequeathed the 283 Monroe Street property to Rachel Haggerty, wife of John Haggerty, of the City of New York.

Who were these three beneficiaries and how did John come to know them well enough to include them in his Will? Annette Ferris was born on May 31, 1844. Her maiden name was Annette Stowe. Still no discernible connection between Annette Ferris of Lamartine, Wisconsin and John Hooper. Annette's mother married Cyrus Stowe. Still no connection. However her mother's full maiden name was Hannah Maria Hooper Stowe. Hannah was born on October 4th, 1827 in New York and may have been a first cousin to John. Her parents were Peter V. Sang of Germany and Maria Hooper. On September 25, 1845 Hannah Marie Hooper married Cyrus Stowe in Lamartine, Wisconsin. She had five children including Annette Stowe. And that's the apparent connection. Adding to this bit of ancient family history was that Annette's son George had the middle name, Hooper.

With Annette's connection now better understood, the second mystery legatee, Amelia Redfield was Annette's younger sister. She was born in 1847 and later attended Lawrence University in 1864 before marrying Rodney Redfield. They had six children and upon Amelia's death, those children then living would have inherited the property at 287 Monroe Street. They may not have even known John Hooper or anything about Brooklyn, but they would now own this property. Yes, John had cast a wide net among family to share in his wealth, including far off Minnesota and Wisconsin.

His final non-charitable bequest was yet another mystery beneficiary, Rachel Haggerty. All that was initially known about her was that she was married to John Haggerty and lived in New York City. Yet, this bequest must have tugged at John's heart more than the other bequests because Rachel P. Haggerty was the daughter of John and Clarissa Horton and was the late Angeline Hooper's sister. Rachel was born in April 1825. It is also clear how close they were as siblings. Rachel (who married twice) named her daughter Angeline Louisa after her sister.[183]

John was given some solace that Angeline's sister was close by. His gift to her was the brownstone in Brooklyn at 283 Monroe Street, a bequest to Rachel and her heirs, forever.

A BEQUEST TO HIS SON

Benjamin Franklin Hooper had to wait until the twenty-sixth paragraph to fully understand his father's magnificent bequest. Benjamin would receive all of John's stock in Colwell Lead. But paragraph twenty-seven also included the golden residuary clause. Specifically any property not otherwise distributed went to the estate's trustees "to collect

---

[183] *New York Historic Homes and Family History, Volume 2*, page 375

and receive the rents issues, income and profits hence arising and to pay over the same semi-annually unto my son Benjamin F. Hooper during the term of his natural life and at his death the said trust shall cease". All the trust property would then be "conveyed, divided and distributed to, between and among the lineal descendants of my said son Benjamin F. Hooper" who were then living would receive equal portions.

It was clear that John's initial intent was to preserve the largest portion of his estate by directing it to his son and his family. John ensured that Benjamin would become an instant millionaire, with his progeny also sharing in his great wealth. What could go wrong? Time would tell. But first John and his magnificent charitable legacies.

John Hooper

CHAPTER 14

A Penumbra of Hope

He who has compassion on the poor lends to the Lord, and
He will repay him for his good deed.[184]

What was the City like in the 1880's? Much has been
examined, researched, and written about the under-class and
even those without a rung on the class-ladder. With
smidgeons of great wealth, it was also clearly a time of great
poverty, homelessness, and child-neglect. Extremes in
temperature led to childhood sickness and death. As
explained in one account:

> In extreme warm weather the heat is a severe trial; to
> tenement children. Their constitutions are not fitted to
> endure the strain, and many of them succumb. They live in
> those sections where the heat is felt the worst, and where
> there is the least chance to escape from it.[185]

[184] Proverbs 19:7.
[185] *The Brooklyn Daily Eagle*, July 22, 1900.

Combatting heat fatigue, homelessness, hunger, ignorance, little girls forced to take on responsibilities of child rearing, and so much more, many concerned adults and their organizations, some newly formed, stepped into the breach. John's final gifts helped countless children and others struggling with poverty.

To this end, John bequeathed the sum of $5,000 to fifteen New York City/Brooklyn charities. Most were to benefit children, but others, such as *The Society for the Prevention of Vice* or *The Society for the Prevention of Crime in the City* were to improve the "general welfare" of the community. One gift was given outright to a church: *The New York City Church Extension and Missionary Society*.

SPECIFIC CHARITIES

First on John's list was *The Children's Aid Society*. As described in one account "[t]he practical value of the work of this society cannot be fully estimated, but there is no doubt that it has been largely instrumental in the decrease of juvenile crime and vagrancy..."[186] And right to the point about summer's heat, the Society dispatched physicians into the tenements. This branch of the *Children's Aid Society* was bluntly named the *Sick Children's Mission*. "Nourishing food and medicine are furnished by this branch...to the utterly destitute without cost."[187]

---

[186] *The New York Times*, November 26, 1890.

[187] *The New York Times*, July 5, 1892.

When not combing the tenements to save lives, members of the *Society* were busy hosting thousands of children, composed chiefly of little girls attending the Society's industrial schools. These children spent up to a week at Summer House on Bath Beach.[188] And unbeknownst to any of these little ones, John Hooper played a part in furthering the successes of the Society.

John's second charitable bequest was made to the *Association for Improving the Condition of the Poor*. Like the *Children's Aid Society*, this organization could not solve poverty or eradicate hunger, but it could make a dent by providing generous help to as many children as funds allowed.

This $5,000 contribution went, in part to Vacation Schools. At first glance the notion of attending summer school is anathema to most juveniles, a point taken in a wonderfully written, tongue-in-cheek article about the drudgery of attending any school.[189]

The writer describes his own experiences with "preparatory discipline." Was it even possible that a school program can be more than just strict and foreboding? Our writer exclaims: EUREKA, "I have seen it. I have found it in the vacation schools of New York City, as [organized] by the *Association for Improving the Condition of the Poor*".[190]

---

[188] *The New York Times*, June 12, 1895.
[189] *Harper's Weekly Journal of Civilization*, September 7, 1895.
[190] Ibid.

Eureka indeed. Perhaps taking a page from the *Little Mother's Aid Association*, vacation school included "fun", such as dancing, learning how to sew, or physical education, to name a few.

Vacation Schools *(Harper's Weekly Journal of Civilization,* September 7, 1895)

The summer programs took much of the sting out of the dreaded term *pedagogy* complained of by the *Harper's* writer, and in no small part thanks to John Hooper.

John had been a director of *The Brooklyn Society for the Prevention of Cruelty to Children*. This organization would also reap a $5,000 legacy to aid in meeting the needs of neglected children. Prevention of cruelty? What an unpleasant, but plainly stated reality of those times. The shame of that every-day occurrence wasn't routinely ignored, but was firmly dealt with by this impressive charity. Indeed, John was well aware of this mission as a board director and friend of this society. An 1884 piece describes in harrowing detail the fear the little ones faced:

> A brutal and exacting father excites hatred and dread in the hearts of his little ones...the number of innocent and helpless who are beat and abused by drunken and heartless parents is very large is shown by the fact that 653 complaints of cruelty and neglect were lodged [at the Society].[191]

As disturbing as the cold statistics memorialize, John would have been anxious about what this might portend. In the midst of this great affluence was an uneducated underclass. John would have agreed with the following sentiments:

> Scores of children are growing up in these lower wards of Brooklyn ignorant of their Creator's name, save as they hear in blasphemy. One of our Bethel teachers, not long

---

[191] *Brooklyn Eagle*, February 18, 1884.

ago, asked a little fellow in her class what he knew about God? "What's He", was the reply....[192]

John, as a man of faith, put forward his best effort to help by his work on the board and through this legacy.

It is clear John was laser-focused on these and related issues. John gave $5,000 to an allied organization, *The Society for the Aid of Friendless Women and Children* and to three organizations devoted to orphans. John seemed particularly concerned with orphans that stumbled about the tenements with little to eat and then only at irregular times, wearing tattered clothes, and with little future other than perhaps someday taking from others that which they had been denied. John's big-hearted efforts to help orphaned children may have been because he had also been orphaned at a young age.

In a remarkable piece written about John years after his death, the writer explored John's charitable impulse:

> He was a man of a most sweet and kindly disposition, and with a heart overflowing with sympathy for those of his fellowmen in distress.[193]

Yet, while these sentiments were no doubt accurate, John's multiple gifts to local charities may have been much more nuanced than simply caring for the poor. Could their collective condition be improved, if only slightly?

---

[192] Ibid.

[193] *The Brooklyn Citizen*, November 1, 1896.

John may have been looking ahead, seeing what the great muckrakers of the early Twentieth Century and child labor reformists were also beginning to see. John took it one step further. He was as concerned about the failures of the Gilded Age as was another bright star and nurturer of children, Alma Calder Johnston, founder of the *Little Mothers Aid Association*, who expressed the following:

> When working men and working women feel that the great mass of those who have capital, capitalists, are with them in true sympathy and charity, when they know that capital is helping to make their homes better, their families in improved condition, their little ones cared for, made happier by those who, though blessed with greater riches, stand still their friends and helpers, where is going to be mob rule and strikes and communism? I firmly believe that this grand deep work in which we are privileged laborers is destined to be an important factor in this, the greatest question of the nineteenth century.[194]

John was astute in business and politics. He was looking ahead at a troubled New York metropolitan area, the same one Mrs. Johnston was also surveying. John knew his remaining time was limited. Sprinkling his capital at worthy and successful charities would help these privileged laborers improve the lot of the growing underclass. Perhaps John was not simply making bequests for self-aggrandizement. The record suggests he was making the effort he could make to better others. But for the furor over how he handled the marriage question with Mary and Henrietta, his charitable impulses would have been yet an amazing story in the City's great newspapers to memorialize his passing.

---

[194] Story of the Littler Mother in the Annual Report 1895-96 p. 19.

CHAPTER 15

Lasting Legacy

PART ONE

A fountain where at man and beast can drink.

Paragraph 25 of John Hooper's will instructs: "A fountain where man and beast can drink." John's executors were given $10,000 for the purpose of erecting two fountains: one in New York and one in Brooklyn. John did not want his fountains erected in a park. This would have stilted their intended use. Instead John tasked his executors with obtaining permission from relevant authorities to place each fountain "in some thoroughfare: that the simple stone work of which such fountain shall be constructed, shall bear only this inscription:

Presented to the City of (New York or Brooklyn as the case may be) by John Hooper

This proved to be a challenge for John's executors. They had to coordinate with authorities from both New York City and Brooklyn City. Understandably it took time, given efforts already devoted to the complexities of his estate. Yet they got the job done.

New York City was the first to complete the task. The architect was George Martin Huss. The location was at Maher Circle, 155th Street and Edgecombe Avenue. The base was composed of granite with a bronze plaque. Above this base stood a fifteen-foot tall lantern.

An 1896 *Sunday Times* full-page spread, featuring the Hooper Fountain as one of three, expressed:

> Fountains that give forth cool, sparkling water to the thirsty man or beast are always welcomed by the public. Even if the beholder cannot drink from the grand affair in the parks and squares they are refreshing to look at on a hot summer's day.[195]

Times readers were alerted to this story the day before. Namely, there would be a feature appearing on Sunday: *Water for Man and Beast.*[196]

Congratulations were in store for Manhattan: it had the Hooper Fountain!

Meanwhile in Brooklyn, a comedy of her lesser aldermen metaphorically moving the fountain here and there and then

---

[195] *The New York Times*, May 17, 1896.
[196] *The New York Times*, May 16, 1896.

The Hooper Fountain 1894 (New York Times, May 17, 1896)

back to here played out. It started in 1892. A small article appears conveying that John's executors had called upon Brooklyn's mayor and the Park Commissioner to discuss John Hooper's gift of the fountain to Brooklyn. The writer summed up that it was "quite likely that something definite [would] soon be done."[197] But not really.

On October 2, 1894. Brooklynites were greeted with this headline:

---

[197] *The Brooklyn Daily Times*, February 17, 1892.

THE HOOPER FOUNTAIN

New York has hers—where is Brooklyn's?[198]

After describing New York's fountain and all its glory, the reporter notes the Brooklyn fountain "appears never to have materialized."[199]

More than a year later it was announced that the Hooper Fountain was to be erected at the "junction of Flatbush, St. Marks and Sixth avenue, in front of the Carlton Club."[200] The fountain was designed in "Italian Renaissance style" and would be enclosed in a thirteen-foot circle in diameter and would be comprised of two large basins for the horses and two smaller ones, with cups, for public use. From this base would rise a "stately column" "to a height of eighteen feet above the grade, where it is surmounted with a square cap with ornamental edges."

Each of the basin types had their own means for delivering water. For the larger basins, water was "supplied through ornamental bronze spouts, which are fine examples of head modeling." Basins for the people's use, would have water supplied "from beautiful bronze dolphins, the tails of which extend up the central shaft about two feet. The waste will be carried off by the pipe through the center of the supporting column. Avoiding the making of puddles at the base of the fountain."[201]

---

[198] *Times Union*, October 2, 1894.

[199] Ibid.

[200] *Greater Brooklyn*, April 19, 1895.

[201] Ibid.

What now seemed to be a sure thing, i.e. Brooklyn would finally be getting its Hooper Fountain, crumbled with the lapse of time and a newly installed group of aldermen staring ignorantly at the issue for the first time. Once sections of the fountain began to appear at the site, opposition stirred. It was too big, or would hamper traffic and would bring "idlers and standing teams."

It appears some of this opposition came from the Carlton Club as well as those who thought the fountain was too close to other buildings.

Now for the comedy that only politics can bring to a moving fountain story:

> While the fountain was thus peacefully slumbering was rudely awakened to learn that Alderman Messenger had sought to kidnap and place it at Ninth Avenue and Fifteenth Street, but it had been slyly taken from him by Alderman Clark's amendment, switching it off to the Eastern Parkway.
>
> Yesterday the illegal disposition of it was resumed. The amended resolution, which had transferred it to the Eastern Parkway was rescinded, and Alderman Singleton, whose constituents had awakened to the fact that a large and beautiful fountain for beasts had escaped from them, reintroduced the Messenger resolution, and the much-traveling fountain is temporarily stopping, metaphorically speaking, until the Aldermen meet again, at Ninth avenue and Fifteenth street. Upon the face of it the only place the fountain has been legally assigned to is at the junction of

Sixth and Flatbush avenues, where the people are up in arms against it.[202]

At long last it was finally determined that the Hooper Fountain would be placed "precisely where they found it, at the intersection of Sixth Avenue, Flatbush Avenue, and St. Marks avenue."[203] The vigorous protests of the past June would give way to joy when "they see the fountain erected and in operation...There is plenty of room for it and the work itself was the design of an architect of recognized attainments." This would not be a "sham or claptrap affair but a handsome work of art...."[204]

And indeed it was. The silly saga resulting from John's bequest to the City of Brooklyn finally ended when Mayor Wurster formally accepted the gift:

> DEAR SIR— I hereby acknowledge the receipt of your letter of January, 8, 1897, stating that you and Mr. Milne, executors of the estate of John Hooper, formally turn over the custody of the city of Brooklyn the fountain erected at the corner of Sixth and Flatbush avenues....
>
> Permit me on behalf of the city of Brooklyn, to tender hearty thanks to you for this noteworthy gift for the ornamentation of our city and to express hope that it will long stand as a memorial of the generosity and public spirit of the giver.[205]

---

[202] *Times Union*, September 29, 1896.

[203] *Times Union*, October 6, 1896.

[204] Ibid.

[205] *The Brooklyn Daily Times*, January 11, 1897.

The *Brooklyn Citizen* gave its own glowing review of this "beautiful work of art" and in doing so painted a gentle review of John's life and included a sketch with his signature:

The Brooklyn Citizen November 1, 1896 (Sketch From Photograph Taken in 1880s.)

Sadly, the Hooper Fountain in Brooklyn is long gone after falling into disrepair and neglect. This is an unfitting epitaph to John Hooper whose name was prominently placed on the fountain and did so much for Brooklyn in the few short years he resided there. Fortunately, John's legacy thrives in New York City near *Jackie Robinson Park*. While that fountain suffered from vandalism, it was restored and remains vital to this day as a prominent piece from New York's Gilded Age.

And its plaque still remains prominently on the fountain just as John had requested:

The restored Hooper Fountain,
Maher Circle NYC (NYC Dept. of Parks &
 Recreation) Granted Landmark Status in 1992.

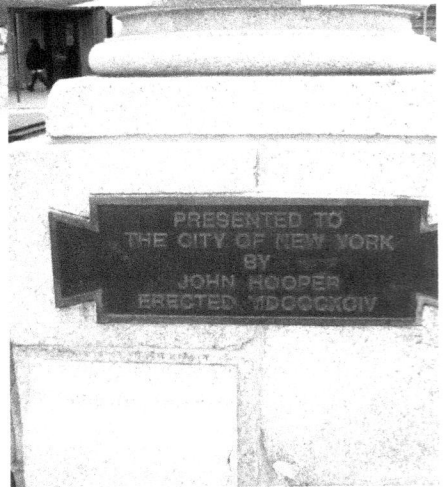

CHAPTER 16

Lasting Legacy Part 2

Boast not of tomorrow, for you know not what any day may bring forth.[206]

John's complex estate took years to resolve. His executors, Mr. Milne and Benjamin Franklin Hooper, pushed to provide accountings to the Brooklyn Probate Court, auctioned off real estate at the *Real Estate Exchange* in March, 1891, and performed other sundry duties to finalize John's affairs.

Meanwhile John's children were moving forward with their lives. Benjamin and his wife Edith May welcomed a second child, John Stanley, in 1890. Mary and Henrietta were now aunts for a second time.

Mary Steurer, having been disinherited by her father, showed little interest in the estate issues. We can assume she was rich nonetheless with the love of her husband, Dr. John Steurer. By all indications, she was an intelligent young

---

[206] Proverbs 27:1.

woman embracing her new world. Her days of studying Latin had ended, but she lived in a busy and fulfilling world as was typical in those days, aiding her husband in his growing practice and managing their home, filling it with seasonal floral arrangements. Presumably she had learned this and much more from her mother and was looking forward to fulfilling her own role as a mother.

Mary would not wait long. About a year after her father's death and the scandal of her disinheritance, she had happy news of her pregnancy to share with her remaining family: her brother, younger sister, and her sister-in-law, Edith May, who, as a young mother, must have been exuberant at the prospect of a cousin for her children.

Yes, it is picturesque: cousins about the same age, with their young mothers enjoying a Manhattan summer day. Our young mothers would step away from the racket and complications of their husbands' respective businesses. After all, they would have their children to raise and enjoy together, especially on those lovely summer days:

<blockquote>
Central Park is a summer idyll;
clusters of people under the shady trees and
round-robins of children,
and a line-up of baby carriages—
graceful groupings[207]
—Grace Duncan Hooper
</blockquote>

---

[207] Hooper, R. J. p. 105.

It wouldn't be surprising if Edith May and Mary enjoyed many such anticipatory conversations about their children. However, the promise of time together and cousins at play was abruptly shattered on the summer day of August 27, 1891. Mary hemorrhaged during childbirth and died in her home. The death notice was stark and devoid of context. She was the wife of Dr. John Steurer. Funeral services would be held on August, 30 at her late residence.[208]

Glimmers of her death could only be gleaned from records kept at Green-Wood Cemetery. Yes she died on August 27, 1891, but so did her stillborn twins. Mary's official cause of death was "child birth".

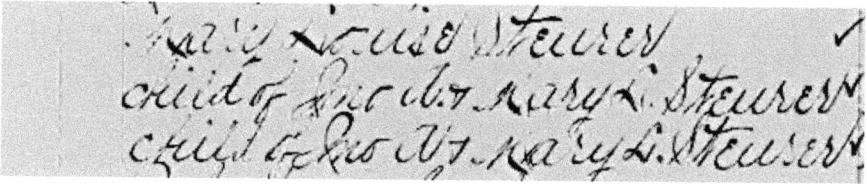

A fragment of Greenwood Record on Mary Louise Steurer and her stillborn babies

Far too soon Mary and her babies rested with her estranged father at Green-Wood Cemetery.

---

[208] *The New York Times*, August 29, 1891.

Burial stone of Mary L. Hooper wife of John A. Steurer; March 3, 1860; August 27, 1891; Located in the Hooper Plot of Green-wood Cemetery, NY

Burial stone of Baby (twins) of Mary L. Hooper and Dr. John Steuer; located in the Hooper Plot of Green-wood Cemetery, NY

Mary left a will dated November 19, 1890. It was only one paragraph, leaving everything but three-hundred dollars to her "dearly beloved husband". The three-hundred dollars was to be divided equally between Mrs. Henrietta Brackett and Miss Mary Brackett.[209]

Dr. John Steurer married again. On February 26, 1898, his wife delivered a healthy baby girl whom they named Mary Louise Steurer. His late wife seems to have been still very much in Dr. Steurer's heart.

Mary's siblings soldiered on. Brother Franklin was president of Colwell Lead Company while his wife Edith was busy with two toddlers and serving as a founding member and finance committee chair of the *Little Mother's Aid Association*.[210] Henrietta was now living with her brother and his bustling family.

Henrietta remained unmarried but may have had a notion about traveling as she applied for a passport on February 11, 1892. The application was completed and witnessed by her attorney William W. Brackett and included a one dollar fee sent to the State Department. The following description was provided for the applicant:

Age: 29	Mouth: Medium
Stature: 5 feet, 4 inches, Eng.	Chin: Small & dimpled
Forehead: of more than medium height	Hair: brown
	Complexion: light
Eyes: Blue-grey	Face: full
Nose: slightly upturned	

---

[209] Mrs. Henrietta Brackett was Mary's aunt (nee Horton), and Miss Mary Brackett was her first cousin.

[210] She was particularly beloved because of her tradition of serving the *Little Mothers* ice cream after their functions.

Henrietta Hooper's Passport Application February 12, 1892. (ancestry.com)

With this fairly detailed description coupled with actual

portraits of her parents, an AI composite yielded the following depiction of Henrietta:

An AI Generated Composite of Henrietta Frances Hooper (openai.com)

Henrietta was an active member of the *Thirty-Fourth Street Reformed Church* and was received into communion of the *Collegiate Church* in February 1896.[211] It is possible she joined this church because her sister-in-law, Edith May Hooper, had been a member since November 17, 1893. And it

---

[211] Catalogue of members in the communion of the (Collegiate) Reformed Protestant Dutch Church of the City of New York.

was even more than plausible they attended church services together since she was living with her brother's family. Aside from her church activities and staying close to her remaining family, her life may have also been one of accelerating frustration as there were troublesome signs of mental illness-mania.

Henrietta was a patient of Dr. Caroline L. Black. Dr. Black attended the *New York Medical College and Hospital for Women, Homeopathic* in 1878. Her type of practice was allopath.[212] As such her practice was considered mainstream relying on drugs, surgery and other conventions.

There is evidence that Henrietta had an appointment with Dr. Black on May 4, 1896. She brought with her a *Last Will and Testament* also dated May 4, 1896. Henrietta signed the document. Dr. Black and Helen A. Woodruff signed as witnesses to the instrument and would later affirm before the Surrogate Court that Henrietta was competent to make a will.

Five days later, Henrietta Frances Hooper died. It had been a lovely Saturday with a weather forecast of "fair and warmer".[213] Her death notices were devoid of detail and simply stated "she died suddenly".[214] Her funeral would be held at her brother's residence, on Monday evening at 8:30.

---

[212] Directory Of Deceased American Physicians, 1804-1929. "Allopath" was the term used for those practicing conventional medicine.

[213] *The World*, May 9 1896.

[214] *The New York Times*, May 11,1896; *The World*, May 11, 1896.

Other than the death notices, there was no other news surrounding her unexpected death except for the records kept at Green-Wood Cemetery. Those records reveal she was thirty-three years old and was living with her brother at 120 West 74th Street in the City. But she did not die at the residence or in a hospital; she died at the *Hotel Marlborough* in New York City. The cause of death was listed as "mania".

Hotel Marlborough 1900-1910 (Library of Congress)

The Marlborough Hotel had opened eight years earlier in 1888 and was located on 36th Street and Broadway. Known for its style, indoor plumbing, and four-hundred rooms, the hotel offered itself as a "family hotel" which meant that most residents stayed long term. In Henrietta's case it would appear her stay was not booked as *long term* but *transient*. What prompted her decision to lodge at the Marlborough? It may have been her illness.

Her diagnosis of mania doesn't suggest a cause of death but perhaps a triggering symptom. She probably suffered from depression. Presumably, she was well cared for by Dr. Black who may have prescribed a medication to calm her symptoms. But the sad fact is she appears have been anticipating her death by executing her will and a few days later checking into the Marlborough Hotel where she then suddenly died. It may well be that she may have taken her own life. A hotel offered privacy and was just such a location where some young women would commit suicide. For example, just prior to Henrietta's death a young woman checked into a different hotel and killed herself with her handgun. Her note indicated she suffered from "hereditary insanity".[215] And there was the curious suicide of a Mrs. Harris, apparently homesick and suffering from a long illness. She entered the Marlborough Hotel having ingested arsenic and also had tried to stab herself. [216]

For Henrietta, she was young and apparently alone when she died. Her funeral was attended by her brother and his wife, close friends, her cousins and perhaps her doctor. Her will was later admitted into probate. She bequeathed to her "loved brother Benj. F. Hooper" all her estate both real and personal, with the exception "of a mortgage on some Seattle property for one thousand dollars" which she gave to her "beloved cousin Mary A. Brackett". "This odd Seattle asset was pursued in the King County Court in Seattle with one I. P.

---

[215] *The World*, May 9, 1896.
[216] *The New York Times*, January 21, 1893.

Taylor having been appointed administrator to sell and disburse the net proceeds to Mary Brackett."[217]

Two sisters and two tragic deaths both within ten years of Angeline's unexpected death. Would their mother have made a difference? Probably not for Mary, but perhaps Henrietta would have found support from her mother.

Henrietta and her mother enjoying tea.
AI Composite (openai.com)

By the end of 1896, only Benjamin F. remained from what had been only recently a family of five. Benjamin and Edith now had three children. (Franklin Walker was born in 1894) A fourth child, John, was born in 1897 but tragically died in 1898. Finally, Grace Duncan was born in 1899.

---

[217] The *Post-Intelligencer,* March 27, 1897.

Benjamin Franklin Hooper

Benjamin continued to serve as president of Colwell Lead Company until his untimely death on April 20, 1902. He was about 45 years old. Cause of death: embolism.[218]

As with his sisters and his father, Benjamin left a lengthy will. He was generous to long-term employees giving each $200.00. He provided a substantial trust ($50,000) to Henrietta who had predeceased him. Like his sisters, Benjamin also left a legacy to his cousin Mary Brackett and the residual of his estate to be held in trust for his widow, Edith May Walker Hooper with remainder to his then-surviving children. His executors were his father-in-law Alva S. Walker, and his friend William Milne.

---

[218] Green-Wood Cemetery records.

Interestingly, he also bequeathed to his wife, Edith May, all his "household furniture, both useful and ornamental, pictures, silver, plate, and wearing apparel, wines, and other household stores, and all of my personal effects of every kind, and all my horses, carriages, harness and stable equipments."

As with Henrietta's will, his will also had a Seattle connection which required opening probate in the King County Superior Court on January 7, 1903. Again, the court appointed I.P. Taylor as executor. The Seattle property was real estate described as follows:

> All of Lot (13) thirteen of block number (174)…of Gilman's
> Addition to the City of Seattle

The property was valued at $1,200 and would be sold with net proceeds to his estate.

Benjamin's death left his young widow with four children, the oldest being about fourteen years old and the youngest only three.

There is evidence that one way Edith continued on with her children was extensive travel by ocean liner. One memorable trip occurred in 1906. Edith and family board the *Minneapolis* in London with an arrival date of September 10, 1906, in New York. A mere eleven years later, the *Minneapolis* was impressed to carry troops during World War 1. She was torpedoed on March 23, 1916, by a German submarine. She later sank while under tow. This beautiful ship was only sixteen years old when she sank. Twelve of her crew were lost. Edith and her children may have been aware of the loss of their ship.

Benjamin and Edith's four children were John Hooper's only grandchildren. Fortunately they were enough to ensure that John's legacy would yield a tremendous abundance in numbers, fortunes, the arts, kindness, and compassion.

This legacy started with Emily May Hooper. Emily was the eldest and more than merely an heir to a large fortune. Yes, she was a debutante as befitting her family's status. In December 1908, "Emily May was assisted in the receiving line by other young ladies, and all enjoyed dinner and a theatre party at her mother's Manhattan home."[219]

Her debutante days were short-lived as she became committed to the burgeoning *suffragette* movement and quickly rose to become an active leader working to secure voting rights for women. And perhaps mirroring her mother's penchant for providing ice cream on summer outings for *Little Mothers*, Emily hosted an ice cream social at Central Park for five-hundred children. These children would soon learn that "*votes for women* means ice cream and yellow lemonade."[220] The "affair was under the direction of Miss Emily Hooper, leader of the 15th Assembly District..."[221]

Emily apparently excelled as leader as attested to in the following headline:

SUFFS HONOR MISS HOOPER

[219] Hooper, R. J. p. 27.
[220] *New-York Tribune*, July 2, 1916.
[221] Ibid.

Yes, there was a large turnout at the *Crystal Room* at the Ansonia Hotel for the purpose of honoring one of their own: Miss Emily Hooper.

The *Votes for Women* campaign came to a successful close with passage of the 19th Amendment on August 26, 1920. With this behind her, it was reported that Emily went on to try and organize retail workers at F.W. Woolworth's.[223] She thereafter wound up living on a small farm in New Jersey and died on November 2, 1953.

Emily's younger brother, J. Stanley Hooper, followed a different path. He was a renowned concert pianist who accompanied prominent musicians such as Albert Spalding, and Julies Friedmann, both violinists. Stanley was also the manager of various events held at Aeolian Hall which promoted concerts with well-known pianists.[224]

Of course, advertising was used to promote these events including those appearing in John Hooper's old favorite, the *New-York Tribune*.

Advertisement for Piano Recital by Max Kotlarsky arranged by John Stanley Hooper (New York Herald, March 18, 1921)

Stanley also spent a great deal of time in Hunter, New York, nestled in the

[222] *The Sun*, December 24, 1917.
[223] Hooper, F. W. p. 37.
[224] *The Chat*, March 22, 1924.

*Advertisement For Daniel Wolf
Piano Recital managed by
John Stanley Hooper (The New
York Tribune November 26,
1922)*

Catskill Mountains, about 131 miles due north of New York City. This was home to Stanley's *Dream Garden*. Elaborately designed and ornately landscaped, it was truly the stuff of dreams for City Society seeking a classical naturalistic setting. It was the trip *du jour* for social clubs throughout the region. One such group journeyed to the

> "...Dream Garden of Mr. Stanley Hooper, celebrated throughout the mountains as one of their beauty spots, for an open-air poetic pantomime, the chief feature of which was the interpretive dancing on the green and the singing of Mr. Fredrick Baer."

Tea was served in the Rose Garden and on the terraces.[225]

There were many other such visits during the Dream Garden's run. Stanley would also serve an annual picnic for family and friends, including concert pianist Max Kotlarsky

---

[225] *Brooklyn Life and Activities of Long Island Society,* September 6, 1924.

and his wife Aida. It is surmised the Depression effectively shuttered the *Dream Garden*.[226]

John Stanley Hooper led a full life and died in 1972. But his love for art and classical music and his passion for creating lavish landscapes was also shared by his younger sister, Grace Duncan Hooper.

What was this youngest grandchild of John Hooper but a composite of a liberated woman of the first decades of the Twentieth Century. She attended the best schools, Brearley, a private school for girls; and Barnard College, the sister school of Columbia University. She completed a journalism degree from Columbia, one of the first women graduates of the new co-ed School for Journalism. With her soon-to-be life-long partner, Florence Levine (aka Ruth Florenz), they were off to the Roaring Twenties, celebrating their young lives as actors at the *Neighborhood Playhouse*. She eagerly participated in the *Russian Teahouse* craze by opening her own version called the *Shipwreck Inn*. Catering to both Barnard and Columbia students and faculty, the *Shipwreck Inn* also hosted up-and-coming poets of the time including a young poet named Langston Hughes.

As Grace's energetic life moved forward she was playwright, poet, and storyteller. One of her plays won an honorable mention at the *Maxwell Anderson Award* of 1938 held at Stanford University. Her play, *Strange Futurity,* was a three-act play steeped in Greek mythology.

---

[226] Hooper, F. W. p. 45.

Throughout her life, Grace amused others with her simple self-deprecation. In a letter written to her brother in the 1960s, she noted she had been awarded third honorable mention in a sonnet contest in Kentucky. She wryly observed "[d]oes that mean there are 2 better poets than me."[227] Grace passed away in 1979 and leaves behind a treasure trove of her writings.

Thankfully, Benjamin and Edith's four children lived through adulthood, or John Hooper's story would have ended. Their son, Franklin Walker Hooper, received an Ivy League education at Yale University, graduating in 1915. He pursued a career in finance and married Marie Louise Sanchez. Together they had two sons: Franklin Walker Hooper and Robert Sanchez Hooper. And from these modest beginnings, John's progeny would explode with numerous great-great grandchildren and many more to follow.

Of course this story is not about his progeny, especially after his own children's lives. Nonetheless John Hooper's legacy continues more than 200 years after his birth on September 19, 1816. And for that we are all grateful!

---

[227] Hooper, R. J. p. 135.

Epilogue

A good name is more desirable than great riches, and high
esteem, than gold and silver[228]

John Hooper began his will "In the name of God, Amen."
In doing so, he committed the financial gains accumulated
over his remarkable life to numerous worthy causes doing
God's work. He did this without hesitation. Evidently, his
charitable impulses ran deep in his soul.

Perhaps this was because he was suddenly orphaned when
his father George Hooper died. He was probably not
pauperized as a result but he was thrust into an early
awakening that life can throw anything at you no matter how
young. And as young John labored forward with education
from Burr Seminary, the Troy Polytechnic and of course West
Point, John would venture from an early opportunity with his
brother at the *Troy Budget* to try his hand at building the Erie
Railroad. It was John's ability to radically shift gears and
adeptly manage multiple diverse interests that eventually led
to his great successes.

Early on, he returned to New York City where presumably, he could have continued with his engineering work. Instead, we find him in the newspaper business, joining the ranks of Horace Greeley at Greeley's *New York Tribune*. It turned out to be a beneficial collaboration. John started with a simple business model of selling advertising, and through honest dealings, hard work, and patient deliberations, became a national advertising business. It was the first of its kind and led to many open doors and wealth.

While John was growing this business, he fell in love with Angeline Louisa Horton, she of rich Colonial heritage and social standing. A wedding on New Year's Eve led to a marriage that would last more than 36 years.

And with the beginnings of a family life, John continued both business and political pursuits. He successfully tried his hand at founding and growing a bank until he was dispatched by the board of trustees a decade later. Meanwhile his three children were growing up before his eyes, with son Benjamin Franklin completing college, and Latin scholar Mary completing her curriculum at the Normal College for Girls.

John's political weathervane seemed to change with the prevailing winds of the time. First a Whig, then a Republican, and finally a Greenback. Meanwhile he sold his advertising business to concentrate on Colwell Lead Company.

John's rich love for his charities continued throughout his life, even after Angeline's death in 1885. John was almost seventy-years old at the time of her passing. Yet, he moved to Brooklyn and by all accounts continued with his busy life, even adding a stint on a charity board.

With all of this success, John then did something perplexing. It appears that he stubbornly interfered with his daughters' courtships, even while blessing his son's marriage to Edith May Walker in 1888. There is evidence that he took Mary and Henrietta to Saratoga Springs with him for a six-week stay at the elegant Kensington Hotel. Why would John suddenly seek such a long vacation from his active business and political life? Was it a furtive attempt to thwart the girls' romantic relationships? We'll never know. However, the situation with his daughters seemed to worsen after that.

Once back in Brooklyn, we can surmise that John didn't bend, he didn't even budge. Mary and Henrietta would be free to marry, but John would disinherit them for doing do. He spelled that out in his first will. Henrietta, his youngest, yielded to her father's wishes and ended a courtship that many believe would have led to marriage.

Mary refused to abide by her father's wishes and married Dr. John Steurer. John then rewrote his will. Mary was still out, but Henrietta would receive income from a trust.

After John's death, the newspapers seized on this story. Of course they would, it captured the public's attention, from coast to coast. But the real story was John's lasting generosity. As again noted in one obituary "[I]t was his invariable custom at Christmas time to send a check to each of the charitable organizations in this city."[229]. Indeed "[o]ne of the last acts of his life was to draw a number of checks for various charitable institutions to which he was a regular contributor."[230]

FREDRICKS.   770 BROADWAY, N. Y.

John Hooper left a lasting legacy with his bequests which helped lift many to a better life. He also left a living legacy with the Hooper Fountain standing prominently near Jackie Robinson Park in New York City. And finally, while John's

---

[229] New York Times, December 23, 1889.
[230] New York Tribune, December 23, 1889.

daughters died tragically young, he still left an ongoing legacy through his progeny that continues to this day.

So to answer the question was he *willful* or *heartbroken* when dealing with his daughters, it seems the results are mixed. It may be that John did not fully recover from the loss of Angeline who possibly helped make him the generous benefactor that he was. He continued with this generosity but evidently lost the gentle touch with his daughters that Angeline would have insisted upon. We can presume he did it out of a stern love, perhaps one anchored in the times of late 19th-Century New York City.

John lived in tumultuous times and he rode the whirlwind well. He achieved great things with little to start out with other than his pluck. Not bad for an orphan who "carried his office in his hat."[231]

(signature: John Hooper)

---

[231] Forty Years An Advertising Agent, page 141.

APPENDIX I

The Family Photo Album

Part I

John and Angeline Hooper and their children

John Hooper (ca 1850s; oil painting in gilt frame; artist unknown)

Angeline L. Hooper (ca. 1850s, oil painting in gilt frame; artist unknown)

Benjamin Franklin Hooper

*Mary Louise (Hooper) Steurer ca 1888, AI-
generated photograph based on family images
(openai.com)*

Henrietta Frances Hooper ca 1888, AI-generated photograph based on family images and passport application description (openAI.com)

Photo Album Part Two

Grandchildren of John and Angeline Hooper

Emily Hooper (Hooper, F.W. p. 49)

John Stanley Hooper (Hooper, F.W. p. 56)

Franklin Walker Hooper ca. 1940s

Grace Duncan Hooper ca. 1910

APPENDIX II

John Hooper Timeline

Sep 19, 1816	Born September 19
c. 1823	Father George Hooper dies
1833-1835	Attends Burr Academy
c. 1836	Attends Troy Polytechnic Institute
Sep 1, 1836 to 1838	Admitted to US Military Academy at West Point (attended until 1838)
1838-1841	Works for Erie Railroad
c. 1841	Joins New York Tribune
Mid 1840s-1870	Starts selling ads; establishes Advertising Company
Dec 31, 1849	Marries Angeline Horton
Jun 30, 1857	Benjamin Franklin Hooper born
Mar 3, 1860	Mary Louise Hooper born
Sep 9, 1862	Henrietta Frances Hooper born
Mid 1860s-1889	Acquires Colwell Lead Company
1866-1876	Founds North River Savings Bank
Feb 26, 1885	Angeline Horton Hooper dies
Nov 16, 1887	John's first will executed
Mar 5, 1889	John's second and final will executed
Dec 22, 1889	John Hooper dies in NYC
Aug 27, 1891	Mary Louise (Hooper) Steurer dies
May 4, 1896	Henrietta Frances Hooper dies
Apr 20, 1902	Benjamin Franklin Hooper dies

APPENDIX III

Letter of Nomination to West Point

Albany, Feby 14, 1835
Addressed to:
Hon. Job Pierson,
Dear Sir,

The undersigned, hereby beg leave to recommend John Hooper as a suitable person to be appointed a cadet in the Military Academy at West Point. Mr. Hooper is a young man of good character and exemplary habits, he has been for two years, a student in the Manual Labour Seminary in Manchester, Vt. From the officers of that institution & from many respectable gentlemen in that vicinity, he has received high testimonials & recommendations.

Mr. Hooper is a young man who lost his father while in his infancy; by that event he was left without a protector, and he has by his own exertion and good conduct acquired a very creditable education. Those who are intimately acquainted with him, believe him to be particularly well fitted to become a member of a military academy. Believing him to (be) a deserving young man, we cordially lend him our recommendation.

Signed:

Kemble (followed by signatures of forty-three members of the Senate of N.Y. and men of note from Troy, etc.)

Dated 25 Feby 1835, Engineer Office

Addressed to:
Hon. Lewis Cass
Secretary of War
Washington
Reference heading:
Recd 23rd of Rep. Feb 21, 1835

Hon Lewis Cass

It is proper that I should transmit the enclosed recommendation to you. I am well acquainted with the subscribers. They are members of the Senate of N.Y. and gentlemen of high standing. They solicit the appointment of a cadet out of my District and out of my state. I presume therefore that my recommendation would be of no avail. I should be gratified if Mr. **Hall**, who represents Manchester, would _____ the appointment of Mr. Hooper.

I am Sir, with great respect

Your Ob't Servant

J. Pierson

Acknowledgements

Thank you, *Meripoint Books*, for encouraging this effort and publishing this little biography.

Thanks also to *the technology of generative AI*, (openAI.com) for processing various pictures, descriptions and sketches of the John Hooper family and providing stunning generated pictures of Mary and Henrietta from a composite of family pictures.

Thanks to Ellen Hooper for dreaming up the title, Fortune, Family, Fracture, for her proofreading skills, and her strong support.

Thanks to Matthew Hooper for input on AI issues and for help with research. His skills are notable.

Bibliography

Eaton, Dorman B. *The Independent Movement in New York: As an Element in the Next Elections and a Problem in Party Government. Questions of the Day*, no. 1. New York: G.P. Putnam's Sons, 1880.

Holley, Marietta. *Samantha at Saratoga*. New York: American Publishing Company, 1887.

Hooper, Franklin W. *War, Wasps & All That Jazz: Life in America During the First Half of the 20th Century*. Bloomington, IN: AuthorHouse, 2003.

Hooper, Robert J. *Born to Responsibility: Remembering New York's Little Mothers*. Williamsburg, VA: Meripoint Books, 2024.

Hooper, Robert J. *Finding Grace: Meandering Through the Life and Writings of Grace Duncan Hooper*. Williamsburg, VA: Meripoint Books, 2023.

Morrison, James L. *The Best School in the World: West Point, the Pre-Civil War Years, 1833–1866*. Kent, OH: Kent State University Press, 1986.

Rowell, George P. Forty Years an Advertising Agent, 1865–1905. New York: Printers' Ink Publishing, 1906.

The Record and Guide, Real Estate Department. "Real Estate Dept." *The Record and Guide* 36, no. 904 (July 11, 1885): 784. J. T. Lindsey, business manager.

About the Author

Robert J. Hooper never set out to become an author, he became one by accident and conviction. When entrusted with the task of preserving the poetry, plays, and short stories of Grace Duncan Hooper, Robert intended only to safeguard her literary legacy. But at the urging of his publisher, he stepped into authorship to tell Grace's remarkable story himself. The result is his debut book, *Finding Grace: Meandering Through the Life and Writings of Grace Duncan Hooper*.

That journey sparked a deeper exploration into Grace's lineage and the world around her. His second book, *Born to Responsibility*, shines a light on Grace's mother and the visionary women of New York City who formed the *Little Mothers Aid Association*, a once formidable but now forgotten organization that supported young girls burdened with the care of their infant siblings while their parents worked.

In his third work, *Fortune, Family, Fracture*, Robert turns his attention to Grace's grandfather, John Hooper, a self-made man who began as an orphan and charity school student and rose to become a pioneering force in advertising, banking, the lead industry, and philanthropy in 19th-century New York City. Through vivid historical narrative and careful research, Robert chronicles John's patient ambition, public triumphs, and private contradictions. At the twilight of the story lies a painful family rift: a father's willful interference in his daughters' lives and the emotional fallout that rippled through generations. Was John Hooper a hard-hearted patriarch or a man undone by love and loss? The answer, like the man himself, defies easy judgment.

Robert lives in Hickory, North Carolina, with his beloved wife Ellen. Their son, Matthew, is a teacher in Boston.

See more at: robertjhooper.com

www.ingramcontent.com/pod-product-compliance
Lightning Source LLC
Chambersburg PA
CBHW041041050426
42335CB00056B/3193